THE

Power of Self-transcendence

THE

Power of
Self-transcendence

An Introduction to the Philosophical
Theology of Paul Tillich

by Guyton B. Hammond

𝕭

THE BETHANY PRESS • ST. LOUIS, MISSOURI
1966

Copyright © 1966 by The Bethany Press

Library of Congress Catalog Card Number 66-19813

Scripture quotations, unless otherwise noted, are from
the *Revised Standard Version of the Bible,* copyrighted
1946 and 1952 by the Division of Christian Education,
National Council of Churches of Christ in the United
States of America, and used by permission.

Typography by David Homeier

Distributed by Thomas C. Lothian, Melbourne,
Australia, and Auckland, New Zealand and by
The G. R. Welch Company, Toronto, Canada

MANUFACTURED IN THE UNITED STATES OF AMERICA

To my parents
who first nourished my
interest in things of the spirit

An Introductory Statement

"THE NEW THEOLOGY," a phrase appearing with some frequency in the decade of the 1960's, has not as yet acquired a clearly defined meaning. Its very currency, however, signifies the emergence of certain discernible trends in theological reflection. Two things can be said about it with reasonable confidence.

The first is that around us on every hand are signs that history has come to one of those rare and momentous turning-of-the-tides in human existence. These signs appear in the new mathematics and the revolutionary physics which have given us nuclear power, electronic "think-and-do" machines, instant worldwide communication, and space travel; in abstract painting, atonal music, and shocking and exciting new forms of drama and poetry; in depth psychology, open-heart surgery, and the "population explosion"; in the ecumenical movement within Protestantism and the Vatican Council of the Roman Catholic Church.

Not since the sixteenth and seventeenth centuries have so many great minds engaged themselves in giving us new conceptual forms in which to articulate new forms of life and thought. Then theologians like Luther and Erasmus, Pascal and Calvin; scientists such as Galileo, Johannes Kepler, and Isaac Newton; philosophers like René Descartes, Francis Bacon, and Baruch Spinoza; dramatists including William Shakespeare and Miguel de Cervantes; the painters El Greco, Rubens, and Rembrandt; statesmen like Cardinal Richelieu and Oliver Cromwell; political scientists such as Hugo Grotius, and many others shaped the ideas and events that rewrote the terms of human existence. The modern age was born.

Now we have apparently come to the end of the "modern" epoch. Mankind travails in a new birth. Every high school student knows the names of Albert Einstein, Niels Bohr, Sigmund Freud, Pablo Picasso, Arnold Schoenberg, and James Joyce. These and others are heralds of a new epoch. The twentieth century promises to be one of the great watersheds of history.

What will this century mean in terms of religious reflection and theological reconstruction? It is as yet too early to answer that question. But all who read and think today are aware that something of tremendous importance is happening in biblical studies, social ethics, systematic theology, and philosophy. One does not need to lose himself in the libraries of the universities and theological seminaries to be familiar with the names of Karl Barth, Paul Tillich, Reinhold Niebuhr, Emil Brunner, Alfred North Whitehead, Martin Buber, Rudolf Bultmann, Jacques Maritain, and Dietrich Bonhoeffer. One meets them in the secular journals and in parlor conversations. Such terms as existentialism, alienation, paradox, encounter, creativity, the courage to be, and religionless Christianity are current literary coinage.

But whatever shape "the new theology" may take, it will owe an incalculable debt to these theologians of the middle third of this century who have already altered irreversibly the directions of theological thought and the terms of theological debate.

This book is one of several to appear with the Bethany Press imprint in the next few years under the general title, "Library of Contemporary Theology." This series of small books is intended to help open doors into this new world of ideas for those nonprofessional theologians of many callings who have neither time nor opportunity to wrestle long and hard with the massive thought of the great thinkers of our time, those whose ideas have already entered into the stream of our religious understanding, and will influence it for generations to come. It is hoped also that these books may serve as introductions to these thinkers and their thought for university and theological students whose special tasks require them to seek some guiding clues to what are often highly technical and dense systems. In any case, the intention is to lead those interested into reading with comprehension the works of these theological leaders who are at the cutting edge of religious conceptualization in our time and whose works constitute new starting points for our understanding of the situation of man in the world before God.

Walter W. Sikes
GENERAL EDITOR

Preface

LIKE MANY OTHERS in my generation I have been helped by Paul Tillich's thought "to remain Christian without ceasing to be a modern man" (in Gerald Brauer's phrase). Too often, however, the difficulty of Tillich's thought places his insights out of reach of the layman who lacks a theological education. My purpose in writing this book has been to bridge the gap between Tillich and the wider audience which could benefit from his writings. Even a partial success in this endeavor would be a source of gratification to me. The task is one which Tillich himself would appreciate: mediation between the thought world of the scholar and the language of ordinary life, attempted by one who stands "on the boundary" (one of Tillich's favorite expressions).

The work of simplification has its pitfalls and dangers. In seeking to lay bare the "skeleton" of Tillich's thought we are forced to remove some of its "flesh." In order to simplify we must eliminate his richness of elaboration. Yet the task must be undertaken even if we risk reducing the profound to the trivial. The reader is urged to use this study as a guide *to* Tillich's thought and not as a substitute *for* it.

I should like here to express my indebtedness to Professor Langdon B. Gilkey of The University of Chicago Divinity School for his encouragement at various stages in my study of Tillich. I am grateful also to Mr. Alfred C. Payne of Blacksburg for making his collection of Tillichiana available to me. Finally, unlike some authors I am grateful to my wife and son for *not* allowing me too much time to be buried in my manuscript. The writer with plenty of time is most likely to lose the one virtue for which the reader is most grateful: the art of brevity.

Guyton B. Hammond

Blacksburg, Virginia
April, 1966

I should that ba... in relation ... ... Professor
Langdon B. Gilkey of the Divinity ... ... Illinois is not
merely the congenial as writer, knows far ... ... Tillich. I
am indebted also to ... ... he read
the selection of Tillich's ... ... with
some ... ...
no one would like to be blamed for my ... ... The writer,
with plenty of clues ... ... likely to hunt the one correct for which
the reader ... ... with the danger of his logic ...

R. C. K.

April, 1960

Contents

CHAPTER I

Paul Tillich's Impact upon American Life

WHEN ONE ATTEMPTS to evaluate the impact of Paul Tillich upon American life, he encounters an unusual phenomenon. Tillich was a scholar who wrote primarily for professional philosophers and theologians; yet he achieved widespread popular acclaim. The great majority of his books make an uncompromising demand upon the reader; yet in spite of this he attracted more public attention than any other Christian theologian of our time. His presentation of his ideas was frequently dense, Germanic, filled with allusions to obscure philosophers of past and present. In the face of this difficulty his lectures drew overflowing crowds, and his words were duly reported in the popular press. A casual count revealed that Tillich's picture appeared in *Time* magazine ten times in a dozen years!

Most of the great figures in American religious life have been "popularizers" (an activity which need not be scorned). The great preachers and revivalists have occupied the center of the stage, leaving the Christian intellectuals largely in supporting roles. Tillich was a definite exception to this pattern. In the search for a precedent to the phenomenon of Tillich's popularity, some scholars have been reminded of the eighteenth-century Puritan revivalist, Jonathan Edwards. Recent studies have shown that Edwards was not simply a preacher of "hellfire and damnation." He was also a philosopher and theologian of the very first rank. In a biographical study Professor Perry Miller of Harvard describes Edwards' first public lecture in Boston. The precise but esoteric language of the lecture, says Miller, must have provoked a question in the minds of his hearers: "What queer metaphysic, or what hidden assumptions, lay behind [these definitions]?"[1] The analogy with Tillich is an apt one. His language too seems to presuppose a "queer metaphysic" which lies behind the scenes. There is, to be sure, no backwoods revivalist flavor to Tillich's work; his tone is cosmopolitan, liberal, ecumenical. But he, like Edwards, is a theologian of the spirit, and if the power of his words is not as dramatically displayed as in the revival exercises, it is there nevertheless.

Tillich's influence has extended beyond the confines of his hearers and readers into the general religious vocabulary of our period. Phrases such as "ultimate concern," "the courage to be," and "the dimension of depth" have become common currency in religious discussions on all levels of sophistication. Although these concepts are not always used in the precise Tillichian sense, their general use indicates the forcefulness of Tillich's mode of expression. In addition, he has aroused the interest of many people (students as well as others) who are not ordinarily attracted to thought dealing with religion. Indeed, Tillich is more than a little responsible for the fact that theology has regained a certain respectability in academic circles.

It must be admitted, however, that this largely favorable reception of the Tillichian message by substantial segments of the general public has thus far been relatively superficial. Few who speak of "ultimate concern" have followed the detailed development of this concept in Tillich's three-volume *Systematic Theology;* few who speak of "the dimension of depth" grasp Tillich's technical meaning. His sermons, it must be admitted, are admirable for their lucidity, and perhaps they have been more widely read.[2] Their full significance, however, can be recognized only in relation to a richly elaborated structure of thought which remains in the background.

When one turns to the more scholarly evaluations of Tillich's work, he finds a striking diversity of opinion, both in the theological and the philosophical worlds. Theologians have experi-

---

[1]Perry Miller, *Jonathan Edwards* (New York: W. Sloane Associates, 1949), p. 32.
[2]Paul Tillich, *The Shaking of the Foundations* (New York: Charles Scribner's Sons, 1948); *The New Being* (New York: Charles Scribner's Sons, 1955); *The Eternal Now* (New York: Charles Scribner's Sons, 1963).

enced a continuing difficulty classifying Tillich's thought in one of the convenient categories used to identify "schools" of theology. When Tillich arrived from Germany in the early thirties, it was assumed that he belonged to the so-called neoorthodox or Neo-Reformation group identified with the Swiss theological giant, Karl Barth. It soon became clear, however, that this assumption was far from accurate. Attempts to associate Tillich with American religious liberalism were equally futile, although some of his views were congenial to the liberals. Since it had been clear all along that he was not a fundamentalist, the categories were exhausted, and attempts to classify him came largely to a standstill. The fact that Tillich himself suggested the term "neo-dialectical" to describe his thought did little to dispel the puzzlement.

Subsequently it was recognized that Tillich uses philosophy in a way fundamentally different from that of any of the schools of theology we have mentioned. The positive role which he assigns to metaphysics suggests a similarity with the medieval philosopher and theologian, Thomas Aquinas. However, the strongly Protestant tenor of his thought makes it impossible to call him a Neo-Thomist. The student of philosophy will recognize that Tillich's philosophical roots lie in nineteenth-century German idealism (especially in the thought of Hegel and Schelling), a type of metaphysics that flourished on Protestant soil. But the fact remains that Tillich belongs to no theological school; his thought is unique on the contemporary religious scene and therefore cannot be classified in any satisfactory way.

Among the theologians who have sought to come to grips with Tillich's work in detail, two different tendencies are evident. There are those who find in his theology "the growing-point of contemporary religious thought."[3] Thinkers like Macquarrie agree with Tillich that faith and culture ought not to become alienated from each other. Faith must seek to find its expression in concepts which are meaningful to contemporary culture. Therefore, they agree that theology must seek to maintain a posi-

---

[3]John Macquarrie, *Twentieth Century Religious Thought* (New York: Harper and Row, 1963), p. 375. Macquarrie applies this phrase to Tillich and Rudolf Bultmann.

tive, dialogical relationship with the philosophy and the other relevant cultural expressions (e.g., art and literature, natural and social sciences) of the age. Although few would follow Tillich slavishly at every point, many who fall into this group feel that he has initiated a number of fruitful avenues for theological development.

On the other hand, there are those theologians who take sharp issue with one or another of Tillich's central doctrinal formulations. For example, Father George H. Tavard marshalls Protestant as well as Catholic support for the view that Tillich's approach to Christology is "deficient, not to say misleading," because "it is not biblical enough, not historical enough, not theological enough."[4] In a more sweeping generalization Kenneth Hamilton concludes that Tillich's system as a whole is "incompatible with the Christian gospel."[5]

Certain of the younger theologians of the "secular" gospel also reject Tillich, but for different reasons. Writers like Harvey Cox and Paul Van Buren hold that Tillich's thought is *too* traditional, especially at the point of Tillich's contention that men are incurably religious even though their religion may take a secular garb. These representatives of the "new theology" maintain that modern, secular man can dispense with religion; therefore Tillich's system is based upon an outdated view of human nature.[6]

This difference of evaluation among influential theologians indicates that fundamental issues are at stake. Some of these issues have been identified, and the alternatives are clear. However, prior to the publication of the *Systematic Theology,* Volume III, late in 1963, Tillich's work was incomplete, and a number of his positions lacked full elaboration. This incompleteness, combined with ambiguities in the earlier volumes, led to conflicting interpretations of some features of his thought. Only in recent days has a thorough theological appraisal of Tillich's work been pos-

---

[4]George H. Tavard, *Paul Tillich and the Christian Message* (New York: Charles Scribner's Sons, 1962), p. 167.

[5]Kenneth Hamilton, *The System and the Gospel* (New York: The Macmillan Company, 1963), p. 227.

[6]Cf. Harvey Cox, *The Secular City* (New York: The Macmillan Company, 1965), pp. 78-81.

sible. There is as yet, then, no consensus with regard to his theological achievement.

A variety of alternative interpretations of Tillich's work has appeared in philosophical circles also, for he has proved no easier to classify philosophically than theologically. Recognizing that he has abandoned the thought framework of traditional theism, philosophers have cast about for similarities between Tillich and various philosophical schools. Some see him as a direct descendant of the great nineteenth-century Germany system builder, G. W. F. Hegel. In Hegelian idealism *Geist* (divine Mind or Spirit) is the primary reality; the realms of nature and human history are interpreted as aspects of the process of divine self-realization. Tillich's stress upon the idea that God's nature depends upon man and the world for its fulfillment seems to some to be clearly Hegelian. This identification would tend to make Tillich's philosophical reputation contingent upon Hegel's. And although there has been a revival of interest in Hegel in some circles, the system building with which Hegel is associated is still in philosophical disrepute.

Other interpreters, however, find in Tillich's thought a form of naturalism and propose that for him the idea of God is transformed into a symbol for "the religious dimension of the world."[7] In support of this view one can point to Tillich's strong attack against the understanding of God as a supernatural being. Tillich can find common cause with the naturalism of a philosopher like Spinoza, and he speaks of his own thought as a "self-transcending naturalism." (Of course, it is this feature of Tillich's work which most disturbs defenders of supernaturalistic theism.)

Philosophers also disagree with regard to the ground rules of Tillich's method of philosophizing—his "theory of knowledge." To put the question broadly, does he base his claims for truth as a philosopher upon pure reasoning in one or more of its forms, or does he rely in important ways upon experience or intuition? In reply to this query, some have emphasized Tillich's affinities with the antirationalistic and intuitive concepts of existentialism,

---

[7] Cf. this view in John Herman Randall, Jr., *The Role of Knowledge in Western Religion* (Boston: Starr King Press, 1958), p. 124.

while others see in his systematic constructions another version of rationalistic metaphysics in religious disguise.

Diversity in classification is matched by diversity in evaluation. One eminent philosopher, praising Tillich's achievement, asserts that "his is a first-rate philosophical mind."[8] On the other hand, a reviewer of a recent book analyzing Tillich's use of philosophy concludes: ". . . Thomas depicts the features of a man enmeshed at point after point in category mistakes, often incorrect in interpreting his historical references, inconsistent or confused in his inferences. In short, Tillich is presented as an inept philosopher. . . ."[9] In the face of these differences, the layman is surely justified in being a bit confused!

In summary it may be said that Tillich's work has aroused uncommon interest in both the theological and the philosophical worlds. However, evaluations of his work range from the strongly favorable to the sharply critical. In spite of the profoundly creative impetus which Tillich has provided American theological thought on all levels, it appears that negative evaluations have recently been in the forefront of attention. One would assume that more balanced assessments of his full theological and philosophical achievement will be forthcoming. In the judgment of this writer Tillich's great positive contribution to American theology will in time be recognized.

One major reason for the confusion which produces conflicting interpretations of Tillich is the failure of interpreters to come to grips with Tillich's "system," taken as a whole. It is quite apparent that individual concepts in Tillich's thought must be examined in their context, but it is exactly this systematic framework which is not adequately appreciated. A full grasp of the *Systematic Theology* was admittedly difficult prior to the completion of its publication. In addition there has been some misunderstanding of and resistance to the systematic enterprise as such. With this problem in mind we might with profit ask our-

---

[8]Randall, "The Ontology of Paul Tillich," in *The Theology of Paul Tillich*, ed. by Charles W. Kegley and Robert W. Bretall (New York: The Macmillan Company, 1952), p. 161.

[9]Paul Van Buren, "Tillich as Apologist," a review of *Paul Tillich: An Appraisal* by J. Heywood Thomas. Copyright 1964 Christian Century Foundation. Reprinted by permission from the February 5, 1964 issue of *The Christian Century*, p. 177. Van Buren's statement somewhat exaggerates Thomas' conclusions.

selves at this point: What is a theological system in Tillich's sense of the word?

The initial impulse behind the effort to be systematic is the desire to be consistent. As Tillich has expressed it, "in making a new statement, the necessity of surveying previous statements in order to see whether or not they are mutually compatible drastically reduces inconsistencies."[10] For example, anyone discussing theology must avoid making statements concerning a concept of salvation which contradict his own assertions concerning the sinfulness of man. Although a preacher may be forced to observe this rule only if he has a few careful listeners in his congregation, a theologian who seeks to deal in a comprehensive way with the Christian faith has no alternative. About this there can be no dispute.

The achievement of system in the full sense requires a more thoroughgoing application of the rule of consistency. It is one thing to seek the truth and to seek also to be consistent insofar as possible. It is another thing to judge the truth of an idea by the test of its consistency with other ideas already held. This procedure is one version of what is known as the coherence theory of truth. This theory holds that an idea can be considered true if it is coherent with all other ideas already accepted. It is implicit in them, and they are implicit in it. This theory does not seek to determine where we get our initial or fundamental truths. It simply insists that ideas held in one area of thought have implications in other areas. Truth implicates other truth; truths cannot contradict each other.

It seems clear that Tillich makes use of the coherence criterion in the *Systematic Theology*. This point has been made forcefully in a recent full-length study of Tillich, *The System and the Gospel*, by Kenneth Hamilton. The author suggests that a distinction must be made between "systematic thinking" and "thinking in a system."[11] The former applies to any orderly presentation of material. The latter, however, involves the organization and interpretation of material in such a way as to produce a whole which

---

[10]Tillich, *Systematic Theology* (Chicago: The University of Chicago Press, © 1963 by The University of Chicago), III, p. 3.

[11]Hamilton, *op. cit.*, p. 13.

is rationally coherent. This coherence is thought to enhance the intelligibility of each of the parts and thus to produce a greater degree of credibility. Thus a rational criterion is employed to determine the way in which all data are interpreted.

The main theme of Hamilton's book is the argument that "thinking in a system" as employed by Tillich (and presumably in general) is entirely inappropriate as a means of presenting the Christian gospel. This is the case, he believes, because the rational criterion of coherence determines what is the valid content of the Christian faith. Hamilton maintains that Tillich's method can make no place for the central affirmation of Christianity, that we have received a message "by its very nature authoritative—a message from God."[12] Such a message, says Hamilton, by its nature cannot be subject to any rational criterion. Tillich's method incorrectly seeks to incorporate certain Christian affirmations into a general system which is rationally coherent. In so doing he has lost the authoritativeness of the Christian message.

Hamilton's study of Tillich is helpful in clarifying the meaning of systematic thinking, but in our judgment Hamilton is quite wrong in his conclusions. His error seems to stem from a failure to understand the nature of Christian "apologetic" theology. This form of Christian theology goes back at least as far as the second century "apologists," such as Justin Martyr. In simplest terms it attempts to show the nonbeliever that Christian faith can make sense of his (and man's) total experience better than rival world views. Of course the whole matter hinges upon the question of what making sense means. Agreement on this matter may be implicit rather than explicit, but no real discussion is possible unless it is assumed that the two parties do agree upon some form of making sense.

There are, in fact, several alternative grounds for such agreement-criteria for determining whether one will accept an idea as "true." (It is not self-evident that we must use the same criterion in all areas of truth.) No one of these criteria is distinctively Christian; nor is one necessarily more alien to Christianity than

---

[12]*Ibid.*, p. 23.

another. Tillich has selected (at least in major portions of his work—he may use others elsewhere) the criterion of coherence. He says in effect, "Let's take certain fundamental features of Christian experience and by tracing their implications see if a comprehensive and coherent world view can be constructed which does justice to Christian experience without violating other known truth. If we succeed, we shall have formulated a strong defense of Christian faith by showing how all of the pieces composing man's total encounter with reality can be fitted together along Christian lines." This is a daring enterprise, both in the confident assumption that "truth is one" and in the willingness to follow the implications of one's ideas even at the risk of challenging old assumptions. But it is also a courageous form of defense which may succeed impressively.

To be sure, there are other forms of apologetic theology which also seek to make sense in the nonbeliever's terms. One might, for example, prefer the pragmatic test to the test of coherence. If so, he would argue that Christian faith works best in solving his (and man's) practical problems. Once again a criterion of truth (workability) is applied which is not drawn from the faith itself. Apologetic theology would have no function if such agreed-upon criteria could not be found. Probably the test of coherence is less familiar in contemporary American Christian apologetics than the pragmatic test. We are accustomed to hearing that Christianity is valid because it is successful in solving individual and social problems. But this test is no more and no less inherently "Christian" than the criterion of coherence.

No doubt there is a place for a variety of types of apologetic theology. If one enters this realm at all, he must be willing to search for common ground with the nonbeliever. It is clear that a risk is involved in any defense of Christian faith in terms of external standards of truth, but it is a risk which must be taken again and again, not only in order to reason with the nonbeliever, but also for the sake of the believer who must reason about his own belief.

The enterprise of thinking in a system, then, must be vigorously defended. As to the degree of Tillich's success in reformulating the content of the Christian tradition, the time has not yet come for final judgment. One can, in any case, already call it successful in provoking further theological reflection. Traditionally American religious life has tended to stress religious experience on the one hand and moral application on the other. Until recently, it has not sought to cultivate the life of the devout intellect. If Tillich's stimulus should lead to the beginnings of a theological renaissance, this would be a notable accomplishment indeed. The Catholic scholar George H. Tavard has suggested that the appearance of Tillich's system is a sign of maturity in American Protestantism.[13] It is true that the system had its inception in Germany and is not in any major ways distinctively American; yet it did come to fruition in the American environment and in the English language. For this fact American Protestants (and indeed all Christians) can be grateful.

At this point, however, the reader must be warned that Tillich's *Systematic Theology* is an awe-inspiring edifice. Like some medieval castle, it appears designed to ward off any attempts to storm the citadel. It is a complex, many-sided intellectual structure, built upon concepts drawn from the entire history of Christian thought and of the Western metaphysical tradition. One might say that it is Germanic in flavor, displaying that proneness to subtle abstractions for which the German language is famous. But its difficulty rests more substantially in Tillich's uncompromisingly metaphysical categories. It is the language of traditional (and existentialist) metaphysics, more than anything else, which proves a stumbling block to the average American reader.

In spite of the many occasional treatises which Tillich has written, it remains true that most, though perhaps not all, of his insights are rooted in and derived from some aspect of the system. Therefore, those who want to grasp Tillich's thought must come to grips with the three-volume *Systematic Theology*. One of the main purposes of this book is to provide some guidance in this enterprise. First, however, let us pause for a biographical sketch of the man behind the system.

---

[13]Tavard, "Paul Tillich's System," *The Commonweal*, LXXIX (February 7, 1964), p. 566.

CHAPTER II

Biographical Sketch

ON OCTOBER 22, 1965, the voice and pen of Professor Paul Johannes Tillich were stilled, and the theological world mourned the passing of a pivotal figure in twentieth-century religious thought. Reinhold Niebuhr spoke for the whole religious community when he said: "In the hour of his death we join with thousands of Christians in thanking God for his richly endowed life, and for all the creative influences which are bound to outlast his life."[1] Dean Jerald C. Brauer of the University of Chicago Divinity School described Tillich's distinctiveness in this way: "Above all, Paul Tillich made it possible for countless modern men to become or remain Christian without ceasing to be modern men."[2] All of those who knew Professor Tillich speak of his great intellectual gifts, but one is perhaps most impressed by accounts of his willingness, indeed eagerness, to give of his great wealth of experience and insight to his students. Perhaps the finest testimonial to Tillich the man is to say that he was a great teacher as well as a great scholar.

There may be some philosophers whose personal biographies are almost entirely irrelevant to their thought. This is not the case with Paul Tillich. His intellectual development bears the deep imprint of personal experience. Also, his own private history mirrors the dramatic upheavals of twentieth-century Western history. Therefore, it is necessary to have some acquaintance with his life in order to comprehend his thought. This necessity

---

[1] Reinhold Niebuhr, "Paul Tillich in Memoriam," *Union Seminary Quarterly Review*, XXI, No. 1 (Nov., 1965), p. 11. Used by permission.

[2] Jerald C. Brauer's Eulogy, printed in *Criterion*, V, No. 1 (1966), p. 21.

has been recognized by Tillich himself, as well as by students of his work. Tillich has presented his intellectual biography in several different works,[3] and most recent studies of Tillich have included biographical material.[4] The reader is referred to these accounts for documentation and further details, but the essential information must be retold here.

Paul Tillich was born in 1886 in the village of Starzeddel, province of Brandenburg, Germany. He was the son of an Evangelical Lutheran clergyman and spent his boyhood in several medieval towns before his father was called to a position in Berlin in 1900. His early education was humanistically oriented, with an emphasis upon the Greek and Latin languages and cultures. Several influences from his childhood upon his later development might be noted. He early developed a romantic attachment to nature, which was to express itself in a lifelong attraction toward nature-mysticism. The sense of awe inspired by the cathedrals of his boyhood towns gave him a keen appreciation for the experience of "the holy." And, finally, his struggle as a youth against the authoritarianism of a conservative father convinced him of the value of human autonomy and independence.

After the completion of his secondary education Tillich engaged in theological studies at several universities. (In Germany it is easier to take courses at more than one institution than it is in this country.) He presented theses on the thought of F. W. J. von Schelling (German philosopher, 1775-1854) at the University of Breslau in 1910 (when he was awarded the degree of Doctor of Philosophy) and at the University of Halle in 1912 (when he received the degree of Licentiate of Theology). He was also ordained a minister of the Evangelical Lutheran Church in the latter year.

With the outbreak of World War I, Tillich enlisted in the German Army as a chaplain and served in this capacity for four

---

[3]Perhaps the most accessible is his essay, "Autobiographical Reflections," in *The Theology of Paul Tillich*, edited by Charles W. Kegley and Robert W. Bretall.

[4]For the biographical material presented here the author is indebted to the following sources: George H. Tavard, *Paul Tillich and the Christian Message*, J. Heywood Thomas, *Paul Tillich: An Appraisal* (Philadelphia: The Westminster Press, 1963), and Bernard Martin, *The Existentialist Theology of Paul Tillich* (New York: Bookman Associates, 1963).

years. This firsthand observation of the horrors of war marked a turning point in his thinking. He saw that European civilization would be deeply disrupted by the conflict and that there could be no easy return to traditional patterns after the war. Nevertheless, he preserved his hope that the chaos could prove creative.

After the war Tillich began his academic career as a lecturer of theology at the University of Berlin. Here he began his effort to create a new "apologetic theology": a theology which enters into constructive conversation with philosophy, politics, art, psychoanalysis, and sociology. Tillich throughout his life understood his role to be that of a mediator. He saw himself as a man on the "boundary line"—between theology and philosophy, between church and culture, between the social classes, and later, between the Old and the New Worlds. This effort of mediation led him to speak of his theology as "dialectical," which means, in brief, conversational or in dialogue form.

In 1925 Tillich moved to the University of Marburg, where he became Professor of Theology. Here he was exposed to the existentialist philosophy of a colleague, Martin Heidegger. Tillich was deeply impressed by this mode of thought, although apparently he resisted it while learning from it. He had been previously prepared for existential analysis through his study of Sören Kierkegaard, Friedrich Nietzsche, whose work Tillich read during the war, and the later works of Schelling. This philosophy, with its emphasis upon discontinuity and disruption in reality, was congenial to the mood of postwar Europe. But Tillich sought to reconcile it with older ways of thinking. He took existentialism into a growing synthesis which already included elements from Hegel's idealism and from the Lutheranism of his theological professor, Martin Kaehler. Indeed, Tillich's systematic theology had its beginnings here.

During the decade of the twenties Tillich was also exposed to the new theological movement of neoorthodoxy associated with Karl Barth. Though Tillich, like Barth, had been strongly influenced by Kierkegaard, Tillich could not tolerate the sharp separation between theology and culture advocated by the

Barthians. It remained for Tillich to mediate also, later in America, between the Barthians and the liberals.

This decade in Europe was to experience political ferment as well. During the war Tillich had sensed the growing class conflict and had developed a sympathy for the plight of the industrial workers. After the war he became interested in the philosophical and political writings of Karl Marx (as distinguished from Marx's purely economic works). Tillich learned from the prophetic humanism of Marx without embracing the doctrinaire elements of Marxism. Furthermore, Tillich played an important role in the establishment of a political and social movement which was called "religious socialism." He felt that the alienation between the church and the labor movements could be overcome only by an active participation on the part of religion in the quest for social justice. He became convinced that justice could be achieved in Germany only through some form of socialism. But he never shared the utopianism of the Marxian socialists.

Tillich's political and social views, incidentally, evolved without radical change in the intervening years. Unlike many Americans, he did not have an aversion to the term "socialism" as such. However, he came to recognize the virtues of the American mixed economy and acknowledged the inefficiencies of governmental control and operation in specific cases. In personal conversation he indicated that he saw no reason to advocate a full socialism in the American situation. One feels that in the American context Tillich, like his friend Reinhold Niebuhr, would have been classified as a liberal Democrat.

Neither the movement of religious socialism nor any other political party could prevent the Nazi take-over in 1933. When Hitler came to power, Tillich, who was then a professor of philosophy at the University of Frankfurt, was immediately removed from his position. As it happened, Reinhold Niebuhr was in Germany that summer, and he invited Tillich to join the faculty of Union Theological Seminary, an affiliate of Columbia University, in New York City. Tillich accepted the invitation, and in November, 1933, he and his family emigrated to the United States. They became American citizens and remained in this country except for occasional return visits. Tillich in time mastered the English language and did the great bulk of his writing in English.

Displaying that courage about which he wrote so eloquently, Tillich transformed this traumatic uprooting into a creative encounter. He sought to overcome what he identified as his German provincialism by coming to grips with American philosophy and theology. In the course of time he absorbed certain emphases from pragmatism and American process philosophy, although the main lines of Tillich's mature thought were already set before he left Germany. He found the cosmopolitan atmosphere of New York to be stimulating, especially in providing the opportunity for interdenominational and interfaith discussions. He also found the opportunity to broaden his acquaintance with the psychoanalytic movement which has taken strong root in this country.

At the same time, there were inevitable elements of "estrangement" in Tillich's situation. He was advised to steer clear of involvement in American politics until he could gain a degree of perspective. As a result, Tillich never reentered the political arena as an active participant. This situation coincided with Tillich's own desire to devote himself more exclusively to the task of composing the *Systematic Theology*. One suspects that his political interest was called to the fore by the exigencies of the German situation and was never his primary interest.

One could speculate about a more serious form of estrangement. In Germany Tillich could combine an academic career with active participation in the life of the church. In America the academic world is more sharply separated from the churches. Tillich commented upon this fact:

While in Continental Europe the theological faculties were the leaders of the Protestant churches, in American Protestantism the real power was in the hands of the presbytery or the corresponding bodies. Theology is not dismissed, but it is reduced to a secondary role in American Protestantism—a lesson we had to learn.[5]

---

[5]Tillich, *Theology of Culture* (New York: Oxford University Press, Inc., 1959), p. 165. Used by permission.

As a result of this characteristic, Tillich's American years were marked by an immersion in the academic world and its community, with much less involvement in the world of the churches and its community. To be sure, Tillich lectured to church conventions and the like, but his religious life revolved around his academic life. Most of his sermons, for example, were delivered in college and university chapels. In partial compensation for this separation from the churches, Tillich was able to influence, and to be influenced by, three of America's greatest universities: first Columbia University (1933-1955), then Harvard University (1955-1962), and finally the University of Chicago (1962-1965).

In a recent interview this writer asked Tillich what one does after he had completed a theological system. His first answer was, "One translates it into German." Ironically, he experienced some difficulty in doing so! But he went on to say that he hoped to write a series of "retractationes" (reconsiderations) as Augustine did in his later years, seeking to take account of major criticism. It is regrettable that Professor Tillich did not live to accomplish this goal.

It is clear from this brief biography that Tillich's life and career bear the deep imprint of twentieth-century struggles and turmoil. Like any other profound theology his thought arises in important respects from his experience. It will be helpful at this point to reflect a bit more deeply on the question: In what aspects of Tillich's experience did he find religious significance? We may begin with a more general question: What type of experience would usually be classified as religious?

In American church life, religious experience is frequently thought of as a special type of occurrence sharply separated from other experiences. Also, it is thought to be primarily individual and private. One form of religious experience which has been influential in American life is that type associated with revivalism. Here the believer experiences a rapture and a transformation under the impact of the gospel message. This occurs in congregational meetings, but also in private or semi-private meditations (as when John Wesley's heart was "strangely warmed"). In either case the event is interpreted as essentially individual; each soul stands alone before God. Moral and social implications may stem from the individual's change of heart, but the saving experience is largely independent of the cultural context. Revivals as such no longer play a major role in the life of the larger denominations, but this general conception of religious experience is still widely prevalent.

It would appear that the experience which contained a religious significance for Tillich was of a different nature. He experienced, not individual judgment and renewal, but the recognition of God's judgment upon an entire culture and of the possibility of renewing this culture through God's grace. That is to say, he viewed the cultural disintegration of twentieth-century Europe as a religious crisis in which all Westerners are involved. Apparently these insights came to Tillich with revelatory force during his years as a military chaplain in World War I and in the immediate postwar years. This cultural crisis, and not individual conversion, is for Tillich the "shaking of the foundations." His insight is that the collapse of finite structures and meanings can and does provide a glimpse of eternal structures and meanings. There can be no doubt that this experience was for Tillich an ecstatic, transforming one, analogous in its impact to the conversion experience, if not indeed more shattering.

There are differences, however, between the two types of experience. Conversion emphasizes individual repentance and renewal. As a result, one might join a church or devote himself more actively to its cause. In the revival form, however, the church did not itself fall under judgment or recognize in any collective sense a call to repentance. Through personal crisis individuals were saved for the church or for a more active participation in the life of the church.

In Tillich's experience, however, an entire culture, and this includes the religious "culture" or the churches, is judged and called to repentance. This criticism of the entirety of man's religious culture understood as a fallible human activity—the prophetic criticism of man's religion—is still an unpopular theme in much of American Christianity although it is thoroughly biblical. Tillich stands in a tradition, at this point both

Roman Catholic and European Protestant, which envisions a close relationship between all aspects of a human culture and the underlying religious "substance" of the culture. Tillich has expressed this view in a frequently repeated statement: "Religion is the substance of culture, culture is the expression of religion."[6] Thus for him religion is both a specific activity within a culture and the underlying substance of the culture. It is in this context that cultural crisis is understood as religious judgment and transformation.

American Christianity, with its traditions of individualism and separation of church and state, has tended to think of religion as basically separate from the general secular culture. This must be qualified by the observation that the churches have sought to influence the culture at specific points (e.g., the efforts toward prohibition). Also, it is true that patriotism tends to take on a religious aura. But separatist and sectarian tendencies have been dominant in the American tradition. Furthermore, Americans have never yet experienced a cultural crisis as shattering as that faced by Europeans in the twentieth century. For these reasons American Christians find it difficult to think of religious experience in connection with cultural crisis, and thus they fail to grasp Tillich's concept of "kairos" (the historical moment when the eternal judges and illuminates the temporal).

On the other hand, that crisis which Americans have thus far escaped in the political sphere (and have overcome without radical change in the economic sphere) may yet afflict us in the moral dimensions of our culture. Americans do customarily associate morality and religion (unlike our tendency to separate religion from politics, economics, or art). Moral breakdown is understood as a religious problem. It may be that we are in the midst of a more subtle but nevertheless growing moral crisis where old forms and values seem to lose their relevance. In this situation the individual moral reform undertaken by the churches seems inadequate. The whole question of the moral

---

[6]Tillich, *The Protestant Era*, trans. James Luther Adams (Chicago: The University of Chicago Press, Copyright 1948 by The University of Chicago), Author's Introduction, p. xvii.

foundations of our culture must be pondered anew. The eternal must be grasped in new categories. No doubt we have yet to feel in its full agony the "shaking of the foundations," but we cannot be blind to the possibility. Whether this occurs or not, Tillich's insights can assist us in thinking about religious experience (both in judgment and renewal) in new and more inclusive ways.

CHAPTER III

Introduction to the System:

AN ANALYSIS OF LIFE
AS SELF-TRANSCENDENCE

WE MUST NOW SEEK entry to the system itself and attempt to discover its ground plan. More than one approach to this task might be devised. One would skirt its periphery, noting the various "positions" at specific points, and only then turn to observe their interconnections. We propose, rather, to attempt a simpler but more risky move: to discover its inner citadel, from which all of the various positions radiate. If this effort succeeds, we shall have gained some knowledge of the heart of the system without necessarily being familiar with every specific part. Later we shall consider a number of these specific points in detail, but the reader should then be able to investigate others for himself.

In more direct expression, our effort will be to discover the central conception which seems to pervade all areas of Tillich's thought. Our study has led us to believe that there is such a conception and that the system can be profitably approached from this vantage point. Any interpretation of Tillich's complex pattern of ideas involves the possibility of misinterpretation, but Tillich himself assures us that such risks of life must be assumed with courage. If we succeed, we shall have simplified the task of comprehending the system's individual parts. Hopefully, this approach will provide fresh insights; it will at least avoid boring the reader with a running commentary on every section of the *Systematic Theology.*[1]

---

[1] Cf. my study, *Man in Estrangement: A Comparison of the Thought of Paul Tillich and Erich Fromm* (Nashville: Vanderbilt University Press, 1965), where this approach is developed and documented.

Let us then for the moment set aside all thought about Christian doctrines. We shall consider these later, but we must first open our minds to the systematic development of a central intuition concerning human life. Let us also for the moment engage in the 'suspension of disbelief" which is recommended in viewing drama. We shall have occasion later to consider the type of evidence upon which Tillich builds. The evidential grounds can be better considered after we have some of Tillich's key ideas before us.

We shall not be far from the mark if we take as Tillich's central conception the idea of life as self-transcendence. This rich, many-sided conception has fundamental importance in Tillich's work. Let us begin our examination of it with a consideration of some of Tillich's definitions of "life." First, he suggests that in common usage the term designates a process in which victory is gained, at least temporarily, over its opposite, death. In this usage life applies only to beings on the organic level which grow toward fulfillment and resist disintegrative forces.

In the thought of some philosophers, however, life has taken on a universal meaning, applying to all beings, not just to living organisms. In this sense, life is taken to mean the movement of beings toward fulfillment of their potentialities in the face of disruptive forces. Tillich shares in this tradition, and in this context he defines life as "the process in which potential being becomes actual being."[2] Even with this universal metaphysical significance, the term still retains the suggestion of the polarity between life and death—a suggestion which Tillich thinks is not present in the otherwise equivalent term, "process."

Other aspects of the idea emerge when Tillich indicates that his concept of life is "dialectical." This term (one of those words which always runs the risk of becoming philosophers' jargon) has its roots in the word *dialogue* and goes back at least as far as Plato. In Tillich's expressive phrase, dialectics as a mode of philosophical reasoning means arriving at "a 'Yes' . . . which is

---

[2]Tillich, *Systematic Theology* (Chicago: The University of Chicago Press, Copyright 1951 by the University of Chicago), I, p. 241.

hardened in the fire of many 'No's' "³—a conclusion reached only by overcoming objections and reconciling opposing views. As a conception of the movement of reality, dialectics is rooted mainly in the philosophy of G. W. F. Hegel. In the Hegelian tradition, ultimate being develops through the emergence of opposites which are reconciled on a higher level (the thesis, antithesis, synthesis triad which is familiar because Karl Marx took it over for other purposes).

In a dialectical approach, life can be figuratively described as a process in which victory is gained over death. In the more abstract language of metaphysics, being gains the victory over nonbeing. But one of Tillich's major objections to traditional metaphysics is its tendency to think of being as a static and inert substance which simply "is" eternally without change. When being is conceived as life, its resistance to nonbeing is viewed as a dynamic, active movement, not a static resting-in-itself. It is a process which develops in the face of nonbeing, drawing that which is not yet (the potential) into being (the actual). This dramatic language has overtones of the modern existentialist movement, but it is undeniable that Tillich's insight has its ultimate source in the dictum of Jesus: "Whoever seeks to gain his life will lose it, but whoever loses his life will preserve it."⁴ In this statement, as in Tillich's more abstract formulations, life is fulfilled by "passing through" its opposite. In Tillich's view life is best understood as a process whereby opposites (or conflicting properties) are combined or reconciled. We shall return to this concept as we proceed.

The dialectical view of life is combined by Tillich with the first approach which we cited. This is done by describing the movement from potentiality toward actuality as a movement from the "already" toward the "not yet" of being. This means that being as life moves out from itself into relative nonbeing in order to achieve its full realization. Tillich refers to this movement when he suggests that all life goes out from itself and

---

³Tillich, *The Protestant Era,* Author's Introduction, p. xiii.
⁴Luke 17:33.

returns to itself.[5] Life can only maintain itself against the threat of death or nonbeing by continually creating itself beyond its own present limits.

An illustration might be helpful at this point. An acorn has the potentiality for becoming an oak. The oak does not yet exist; relative to the actual acorn, it is nonbeing. The acorn becomes an oak only by continually going beyond its actual limits in the direction of this not-yet-being. When it reaches tree status, the acorn has realized its essential nature by going out from its original existence. Tillich applies this scheme, at least by analogy, to the whole of reality.

This dynamic quality of life which drives it beyond itself is identified by Tillich as "self-transcendence." The meaning of this term in Tillich's usage is colored by certain aspects of human experience. Self-transcendence is experienced by man as self-awareness. In order to be conscious of himself, man must in some sense stand beyond or outside of himself. For Tillich, the self-transcendence present in all life (hence, in all being) comes to its fulfillment in man and is experienced as self-consciousness. The acorn can be said to transcend itself, but only in a limited sense which does not reach the level of self-awareness. In man the basic movement of life reaches its fullest consummation. This consummation gives man his most distinctive characteristic: the ability to be at once "subject" and "object," the being which is aware and the existing object of which it is aware.

One further refinement of this train of thought must be mentioned. In his latest work, Tillich suggests a distinction between horizontal and vertical self-transcendence.[6] The former refers to any movement from finite potentiality to finite actuality; it remains within the finite natural order. The latter type of self-transcendence is a movement beyond the finite world in the direction of the "in-finite"; it is the transcendence of finitude. Again, this latter type is more distinctive of man. He is the being who can stand beyond his entire finite being and ask the question

---

[5]Cf. Tillich, *Systematic Theology*, I, p. 234; *Systematic Theology* (Chicago: The University of Chicago Press, 1957), II, p. 90.

[6]Cf. Tillich, *Systematic Theology*, III, p. 31.

of the infinite. In our discussion of man we shall refer primarily to vertical self-transcendence. It should be noted that Tillich sees this feature of life in other beings also to a limited degree. All finite life strives toward infinitude, but only man is aware of this striving.

We now have Tillich's concept of life before us in general outline. In all life there is a process of going out and of returning. This is a dialectical process; being moves out into nonbeing. It is a process of self-transcendence. It can be described also as the movement from potentiality toward actuality, a process of self-creation. We can now add that in all life there is risk and threat and, at least figuratively speaking, self-affirmation and courage in the face of threat. Life is not static being but dynamic confrontation with, and victory over, nonbeing.

All of this may be said of life in its basic structure, according to Tillich. This means that life in any form, perfect or imperfect, finite or eternal, will have these characteristics. If we speak of God as the living God, then we must conceive of the divine life, at least symbolically, in terms of this description. The divine life, then, must be said to go out of itself creatively and to affirm itself dynamically in the face of the threat of nonbeing. God's life, like man's, must be conceived in a dialectical fashion.

When these categories are applied to God, certain conceptual difficulties arise which lead Tillich to distinguish between God's eternal life and man's finite and corruptible life. An analysis of this distinction will enable us to grasp Tillich's concept of the relation between God and man, one of the central problems in any systematic theology.

The central problem arises when the terms potentiality and actuality are applied to God. Life's movement from the potential to the actual suggests incompleteness and lack of fulfillment, characteristics which Tillich thinks cannot properly be ascribed to God. Traditionally, philosophical theology has referred to God as "pure actuality," indicating by this that nothing in God's nature remains unrealized. (Thomas Aquinas' view of God is a prime example.) Tillich holds, however, that in this conception dynamic life is replaced by static lifelessness, and the active quality of the biblical God is lost.

Another alternative suggests itself. Life in God must be affirmed, but God's life must be free of the imperfections of finite life. We can conceive of a life whose going out of itself does not imply incompleteness, whose self-transcendence does not threaten self-identity. In another of Tillich's polar expressions, eternal life is dynamic without contradicting realized form. Tillich aligns himself with those philosophers who have affirmed "the dynamic self-affirmation of being-itself" (notably Plotinus in ancient philosophy, Hegel in the nineteenth century, and philosophers like Alfred North Whitehead in the twentieth century).[7] At the same time he criticizes those who speak without qualification of a "becoming" God. (Perhaps he has in mind such philosophers as Edgar Brightman and H. N. Wieman.)[8] Tillich's approach here is dialectical in the sense that qualities which are polar opposites must both be attributed to God. God's being is dynamic and yet eternally preserves its identity.

It is important to emphasize that this view of God's life is possible because man catches glimpses of such a life in his own experience. It is true that our lives move inexorably from birth, through growth and development to partial fulfillment, then to deterioration and death. Change can just as readily be destruction as creation; usually it is both. Nevertheless, we can imagine a self-transcendence which overcomes the negative aspects of finitude. We have said that man tastes infinity, although he does not possess it; by the same token, he tastes eternal life although he cannot hold it. According to Tillich, there are moments which elevate us beyond the flux of time into the realm of the eternal. Though these are fleeting, they enable us to conceive eternal life. Furthermore, they enable us to see that this kind of life is not alien to us; it is our true being, although we are separated from it. Life, then, is not properly conceived until we view it in God, where dynamics and form, self-transcendence and self-identity, are in perfect balance.

---

[7] Tillich, *The Courage to Be* (New Haven: Yale University Press, 1952), p. 179.
[8] Cf. Tillich, *Systematic Theology*, I, p. 181.

From the standpoint of a comparison with eternal life, further observations can be made about finite life. Tillich suggests that while God's life is "unambiguous," man's life (and by extension all finite life) is "ambiguous."[9] His use of these terms requires some clarification. To grasp the ambiguity of finite life, we must return to the idea of life going beyond itself. According to Tillich, the movement toward actualization is tragically combined at every moment with destruction and disintegration. The creation of a new form means the destruction of an old form; the achievement of a new and broader integration of one's life requires the risk of a temporary disintegration.

Several illustrations of his point may be drawn from different areas. Biologically, birth of the young occurs only through a degree of physical sacrifice on the part of the mother. On the psychological level, repressed experiences can be reintegrated with the total self only by breaking down a limited self-concept. Socially, a greater degree of justice can be achieved only through a partial disruption of the present social order. In general, says Tillich, life is continually threatened by disintegration and death; in the language of metaphysics, it is threatened by nonbeing. Finite life is actually disrupted by these threats, although we can imagine a life which continually overcomes them. Finite life is tragic in that its very greatness (self-transcendence) leads to its disruption.

A deeper ambiguity emerges in the distinctively human realm of vertical self-transcendence. According to Tillich, it is in this realm that human freedom appears. (Once again, there are intimations of freedom on the lower levels of life, but only man has freedom in the full sense.) The concept of freedom is in many ways the crux of Tillich's thought; anyone who masters it will have the key to many doors in the system. Unfortunately, his approach to freedom introduces a number of further subtleties; we shall have to labor a bit more with this intricate pattern of ideas. Once over this hurdle, we can pull the pieces together and then turn to the more familiar ground of Christian doctrine.

---

[9] Cf. e.g., Tillich, *Systematic Theology*, III, p. 140.

Tillich's concept of freedom is inseparable from the idea of self-transcendence which we have already discussed. Man is free in that in conscious thought he can stand outside of himself and look at himself. Insofar as he transcends any limiting aspect of his existence, he is free from determination by it. For example, a man who knows that he is an American can, in a sense, stand beyond his "Americanness" and can judge it. In so doing he can accept or reject the values associated with American life. He is not bound by them, although he may choose to affirm them. In a similar way, Tillich argues, man is freed from his finitude (the limitations of his finite existence) by being aware of it. His transcendence of the finite points him inevitably in the direction of the infinite: "Nothing finite can hold him."[10]

Thus, in Tillich's thought, freedom, self-transcendence, and self-awareness are all closely related. All are rooted in the ability of life to go beyond itself and to become "self-related" (that is, to become both subject and object). Freedom and self-awareness appear only in man, but they represent the completion of a tendency which is present in all life. This interconnection of the three concepts may be illustrated on the level of man's cultural creativity. Through language and abstract thought, man can create a human world above the given natural world. Living in this human world, he can transform himself indefinitely in many directions. He is not confined within the limits of natural necessity, although he can never escape his natural finitude. In other words, freedom and self-consciousness are the basis upon which the entire world of culture and civilization is built.

Tillich's approach to freedom largely bypasses the traditional debates between determinism and indeterminism. Frequently, human freedom has been understood to mean the absence of determining causes. In this sense, one is free if his choice of action is undetermined prior to his conscious decision. The determinists have argued that no such indeterminacy exists. However, Tillich does not use the word "freedom" in this sense. For him, the word suggests a mode of being: namely, independence, separateness, autonomy, individuality. There is the connotation of standing out

---

[10]Tillich, *Systematic Theology*, I, p. 191; cf. pp. 178-192; cf. also Tillich, *Systematic Theology*, II, pp. 31-33.

or standing alone. This view can be related to the traditional debates by indicating that Tillich's position is one of self-determination. Free acts are caused by a self, rather than by some external cause. Tillich is therefore primarily interested not in causation, but in the structure of selfhood.

The understanding of freedom as a separation enables Tillich to view the process of realizing freedom as a metaphysical "movement" of separation. The birth of an infant illustrates Tillich's point. The separation involved in birth is the beginning of independence and freedom, but freedom is not complete until psychological independence of the parents is achieved. This too is a separation, although in a nonspatial sense. Tillich has in mind a deeper metaphysical (and religious) separation which encompasses the two just mentioned and goes beyond them.

The separation which constitutes freedom in the metaphysical sense is, first, the self-separation which we have described as self-transcendence. It is this standing beyond oneself which enables one to be aware of himself as a separate, individual entity and to be aware of his world as separate from himself. In another expression, it is this self-separation which creates the subject-object polarity. Thus, as we have indicated, it is the drive of life to go beyond itself which produces human self-consciousness and freedom and which makes human civilization possible. To be free is to stand outside oneself, outside one's finitude.

There is, however, another aspect of the separation which creates freedom and individuality. We have said that the process of self-transcendence is also the movement from potentiality toward actuality. Self-transcendence may be described as standing out from pure potentiality. (Remember in our example that initially the oak is pure potential. The acorn must move out from itself to begin to actualize its own potentiality.) But what is the ultimate source of these potentialities? The religious, and at least one type of metaphysical, answer is that potentialities have their origin in the creativity of the divine life. Assuming for the moment this answer to be the correct one, how are these potentialities related to the divine life? One type of metaphorical expression, which has its roots in the tradition of Plato, suggests that finite potencies (or essences) may be conceived as ideas in the mind of God. Existing beings through their development strive to copy their eternal "ideas." Tillich refers to this metaphor,[11] but one might judge that it is too exclusively mental to express his approach fully. Perhaps the metaphor of offspring in the womb of the Divine is more suitable, although Tillich does not use it.

In Tillich's conceptualization, potencies are real *within* the divine life as the result of God's inner creativity. But they are purely potential until they go out from themselves *and at the same time from the divine "womb" in which they had their potential being*. The potencies are real in God, but they do not "exist" in the technical sense of standing out or standing alone. They are sustained by the power of God and remain in unity with God.

The realization of freedom, then, means a separation from pure potentiality and from the divine womb. This movement of separation takes place through man's self-transcendence and self-awareness. By standing beyond himself, man becomes aware of himself as a separate individual and thus *becomes* a separate individual. At the same time he becomes separated from himself —his "original" being in unity with the Divine. This separation, then, is ambiguous; we have finally arrived at the ambiguity which arises from man's vertical transcendence. This standing out is necessary for full realization of man's potentialities, but at the same time it is a destructive separation from oneself and from the creative source. It is the tragedy of man's life that he must stand beyond himself in his striving for the infinite, but that in so doing he inevitably contradicts himself and is subject to the destructive conflicts which this entails. Tillich calls this condition "estrangement": the negative consequence of the realization of freedom.

Since the condition of estrangement is the inevitable result of actualized freedom, man in his own power cannot overcome the tragedy of his life. According to Tillich, salvation and reconciliation can be secured only through man's participation in God's eternal life. We have indicated that God's life is represented by

---

[11]Cf. Tillich, *Systematic Theology*, I, p. 254.

Tillich as going beyond itself without contradicting itself; we have further suggested that man glimpses eternal life and sees in it his true home. If man can be grasped by the power of eternal life and elevated beyond the destructive aspects of finitude, then he can be saved and his true nature realized. The reconciliation of man with God is possible, in Tillich's view, because God is not a static infinite being. He is the power of life, the source of the power of being to transcend itself. To be united with God is to gain the unlimited power to transcend the negative aspects of finitude. Both God and man are life understood as self-transcendence. There is indeed only one power of life, the power of God. To be reunited with this power after the achievement of freedom is to gain eternal life.

Tillich identifies the situation where man is grasped by the power of eternal life as "ecstatic" self-transcendence (to be distinguished from the natural and tragic process of life). Tillich here attempts to conceptualize the condition of being elevated above one's individuality without losing it. This can be illustrated in two areas of experience, prayer and self-giving love. Tillich cannot be understood to think of prayer as a conversation between two personal beings, although it might perhaps be symbolized in this way. Rather, one might say that in prayer one rises above his finite individuality and assumes the perspective of God, although without a sense of losing his concrete finitude. He experiences the "eternal now" whereby the flow of time loses its threatening quality. He sees eternal meaning intersecting the flow of time. In self-giving love one is united with another and overcomes the "prison" of his aloneness, but again without removing his individuality. I can unite with another only when I am "beyond" myself. For Tillich eternal life does not negate finite life; rather, it fulfills finite life. Tillich views the concepts of resurrection and immortality as symbols expressing the conviction that finite life can be gathered up into eternal life without being destroyed.

This concludes our survey of Tillich's philosophy of life, his understanding of life as self-transcendence. We have not sought to preserve a distinction between those aspects of the analysis which are presented by Tillich as philosophy and those aspects which are presented as Christian theology. It is our conviction that in this central core of his thought, philosophy and theology interpenetrate to such a degree that they cannot be separated. We must hasten to add that Tillich does not take the approach we have followed. He formulates a method of philosophical question and theological answer, thus preserving a distinction between the two fields. Our analysis bridges this gap; we have dealt interchangeably with material from question and answer. Hopefully, by this method we have uncovered the heart of the system.

The train of thought we have followed has its difficulties for the reader, and no doubt certain aspects of it remain somewhat obscure. These ideas reappear again and again in Tillich's specific formulations; hence, they cannot be avoided. We turn now to a consideration of Tillich's own approach to his material. From time to time the reader will be referred back to this introductory analysis; Tillich's treatment of the major Christian doctrines cannot really be grasped without this background.

CHAPTER IV

Tillich's Theological Method

IN THE PRECEDING CHAPTER we plunged directly into the heart of Tillich's system and sought to uncover its central intuition. We did this without pausing to investigate the general organization of his work or the type of data upon which he bases his conclusions. With his synoptic vision of reality now before us, it will be helpful to consider these questions of "method." How does Tillich know that what he says is true, and what is his general procedure for convincing the reader?

It can be readily observed that Tillich casts his thought into the form of a dialogue between philosophy and Christian theology. The dialogue form has been employed in Western thought over the centuries as an effective way of arriving at the truth. As in actual human conversations, questions are asked and answers given; problems are posed and solutions proposed. Tillich does not personify the parties of the dialogue as did some of the great philosophers of the past (Plato and David Hume, for example). His ideas are presented abstractly, but some of the dramatic quality of actual argument is preserved.

In these conversations philosophy speaks for modern man. Tillich is convinced that Christian thought cannot speak effectively to modern man unless it seeks to answer the questions which he actually asks. No doubt Tillich, like the rest of us, has heard too many sermons which present impressive solutions to problems which no one is aware of having. The answers must match real questions; they must meet man where he really is. Tillich is further convinced that modern philosophy speaks best for modern man. It is here that man poses his unanswered questions most clearly. In Tillich's opinion, the same problems appear in other realms of human culture—in art and literature, for example—but in more obscure form. Philosophy conceptualizes the great preoccupations of man in a given era. It is the most accurate reflection of man's self-understanding.

One may ask why the dialogue was not cast between science and religion. Americans are especially aware of the impact of science upon daily life, and frequently vague questions arise concerning possible conflict between science and religious faith. Are not these questions the central ones for modern man? The dialogue between science and religion is not completely absent from the pages of the *Systematic Theology,* but it does not constitute the major encounter. Tillich believes that science as such does not ask the right questions. By its very method—the method of objectivity—science sets aside the fundamental questions of human existence. Man's inevitable quest for ultimates—ultimate meaning, ultimate value, ultimate reality—is categorically eliminated from the scientific enterprise. But philosophy must and does consider questions of this sort and, in so doing, enters into dialogue with religion.

It can be assumed, however, that philosophy takes account of the genuine questions raised by science concerning man's existence. Philosophy must ponder the meaning of science for human life. Thus if Tillich's dialogue does not bring religion into conversation with science indirectly (through philosophy), it will have failed in its intention. Only a careful consideration of the system will determine whether Tillich has actually come to grips with the central problems of modern man.

This general concept of philosophy is too vague to be very helpful. Let us consider more specifically what Tillich means by philosophy. This can best be indicated by describing the types of philosophy which Tillich calls upon to speak for modern man. These are four in number: metaphysics or ontology, existentialism, philosophies of life, and philosophies of history (especially those of a dialectical sort). We have suggested that certain of his deepest insights are derived from his approach to a philosophy of life. However, all of these types play an important part in the system.

First, Tillich holds that all philosophy has its basis in the metaphysical question: What does it mean to be? Western philosophy traditionally has pondered the question of the nature and structure of being as it is found in all entities which may be said to "be" in any sense of the word. This inquiry is known as "ontology." (Tillich prefers this term to the roughly equivalent word "metaphysics.") It is probably true that although ontology has historic preeminence in Western thought, it neverthless is an inquiry less familiar to the American public than other areas of philosophy (such as ethics, political philosophy, logic, or the philosophy of science). Tillich maintains that questions concerning the nature of reality are presupposed in these other areas, so that ontology remains fundamental even when it appears in disguise. Our very language, and hence all our thinking, involves assumptions about the nature of being. In support of this view, Tillich appeals to a long tradition of thought which includes Plato, Aristotle, Plotinus, Thomas Aquinas, Spinoza, Hegel, and many others.

Tillich's understanding of ontology is further clarified when he asserts that it always stems from some religious intuition. The question of being is not simply a theoretical investigation. Since the philosopher is himself an existing being, he inevitably asks the question about the ground and meaning of his own being. He asks not only Aristotle's question ("What does it mean to be?"), but, in one form or another, Hamlet's also ("to be or not to be"). Although with his mind the philosopher may be a detached seeker after truth, in his being he is passionately involved in that which he is seeking. This quality of ontology leads Tillich to assert that "every creative philosopher is a hidden theologian."[1] Every philosopher builds his thought upon some concrete "ultimate concern." However, the philosopher seeks to set aside his personal involvement and to reach a universal perspective, the standpoint of pure reason. The fact that he never entirely succeeds does not invalidate the attempt.

Tillich concludes that ontology seeks God no less than religion does, although from a different point of view and employ-

[1]*Ibid.*, p. 25.

ing different methods and different kinds of data. In like fashion, religion seeks being no less than ontology does, for God must be the ultimate reality. This congruence makes it clear that ontology and theology must be related, for they seek the same ultimate truth. This connection is affirmed in the statement which Tillich takes to be the initial affirmation in all philosophy of religion: "God is being-itself."[2] In the *Systematic Theology,* therefore, Tillich seeks to engage ontology and Christian theology in a creative dialogue. It must be admitted that in his consideration of ontology he does not confine himself to the modern period but ranges through the entire history of ontological reflection from Plato to Alfred North Whitehead.[3]

Tillich's view of ontology is a traditional one, but we should note that it has not gone unchallenged in contemporary philosophy. There is a strong current of thought in British and American philosophy which questions the meaningfulness of the language of ontology. This criticism was most strongly voiced a generation ago in the logical positivism of A. J. Ayer.[4] Ayer's conclusion that all metaphysical language is meaningless is now regarded as an oversimplification, but the tendency to confine the truth claims of metaphysics within the limits of empirical evidence has continued in positivism and in the philosophies of language. It has been argued that although Tillich intends to deal with modern problems, he has not taken adequate account of this major current of philosophy.[5] Twentieth-century skepticism about ontology raises questions which Tillich does not fully answer. This is an important criticism to which we shall return in our evaluations.

The second current of philosophical thought to which Tillich gives attention is the movement known as existentialism. Indeed, Tillich is frequently identified as an existentialist theologian, although this is a one-sided description. It would be beyond the scope of this book to attempt a full introduction to existentialist

[2]*Ibid.*, p. 238.

[3]Cf. *ibid.*, Part II, "Being and God."

[4]Cf. A. J. Ayer, *Language, Truth, and Logic* (New York: Dover Publications, Inc., 1946).

[5]Cf. Thomas, *op. cit.*, p. 180.

thought, but a few comments concerning Tillich's approach to it will be helpful. When Tillich refers to this movement, he has in mind such nineteenth-century thinkers as Sören Kierkegaard and Friedrich Nietzsche and such twentieth-century figures as Martin Heidegger and Jean-Paul Sartre. He also includes the thought of the American pragmatist, William James, and some elements in the work of Sigmund Freud and the movement of psychoanalysis stemming from Freud.

Tillich sees as the common theme in these otherwise diverse philosophies the effort to delineate "what it means to exist."[6] One might properly expand this condensed definition as follows: Existentialism is the effort to delineate what it means to exist and to be conscious of existing as a concrete individual in time and space, subject to all of the limitations of finitude. Understanding the movement in this way, Tillich terms it "the good luck of Christian theology."[7] This means that existentialism provides an analysis which Christian theology would otherwise have to undertake for itself: namely, the analysis of the structures and tensions of actual human existence.

Described in these terms, the existentialist philosophy seems indistinguishable from other philosophies which deal with man. However, Tillich finds in its analysis a distinctive content, which may be described as the recognition of man's estrangement or alienation. Existential analysis describes how individuals have become destructively cut off from nature, from other men, and from their own potentialities. Impressed by the frequent appearance of this theme in existentialist literature, Tillich suggests that it is the fundamental insight to be gained from this kind of study. He further concludes that by recognizing estrangement, modern man has rediscovered the Christian insight concerning man's tragic alienation from God, from his fellowman, and from himself. Thus, while theology enters into conversation with ontology concerning the nature of God, it engages in dialogue with existentialism concerning man and the problem of human existence.

---

[6]Tillich, *Systematic Theology*, II, p. 25.

[7]*Ibid.*, p. 27.

To take an example, Tillich points to Freud's analysis of the conflicts of human existence. Freud described the inevitable clash between man's innate sexual and aggressive instincts and the socially produced "superego," or conscience. According to Freud, the tension between instinct and repression of instinct is always present in man, and at times the conflict is severe enough to produce an unconscious desire for self-destruction. The best man can hope for is a kind of armed truce between opposing forces. Tillich takes Freud's analysis seriously as an accurate description of some aspects of human life. But it is accurate for man in estrangement—man destructively divided within himself, alienated from God and his fellowman. This is an aspect of man's true condition; if Christian thought is to be relevant, it must speak a reconciling word to this condition.[8]

The third area of conversation between philosophy and Christian theology involves a group known in Europe as the philosophers of life. In this country, similar interests gave rise to a movement known as process philosophy. Not all of these thinkers are widely known. Of the European group perhaps the best known is the French proponent of a theory of "creative evolution," Henri Bergson (1859-1941).[9] Tillich also includes in this category the writings of the contemporary French Jesuit, Pierre Teilhard de Chardin.[10] In the United States most process philosophies are rooted, in one way or another, in the thought of the scientist-philosopher, Alfred North Whitehead (1861-1947).[11] The movement cannot be sharply distinguished from that of existentialism. Tillich includes Friedrich Nietzsche and William James in both movements.

We have already indicated the kind of material which Tillich finds in these philosophies. The central theme may be summed up as the effort to formulate a concept of life or process which can be employed as the basic metaphysical category. Reality is

---

[8]For Tillich's dialogue with existentialism, cf. *ibid.*, Part III, Section I, "Existence and the Quest for the Christ."

[9]Cf. Henri Bergson, *Creative Evolution* (New York: Modern Library, 1944).

[10]Cf. Pierre Teilhard de Chardin, *The Phenomenon of Man* (New York: Harper and Row, 1959).

[11]Cf. e.g., A. N. Whitehead, *Science and the Modern World* (New York: The Macmillan Company, 1925).

dynamic, not static, and living, not dead and inert. We have also suggested the deep impact which this trend of thought has had upon Tillich's own perspective. Actually his understanding of life strongly colors his approaches to ontology and existentialism. As we have seen, Tillich finds in modern ontology the recognition that ultimate reality must be conceived in terms of the life categories. It must be viewed as the source of the power of being to transcend itself in the life process.

Tillich also interprets existentialism within the framework of his philosophy of life. According to him, to exist means to "stand out of" mere potentiality. Analysis of existence is analysis of this "standing out." This separation from potentiality, as far as man is concerned, rests upon freedom and self-consciousness. The analysis of man's self-separation inevitably discovers estrangement, for this is part of the process of life—the process of going out from itself and returning to itself. Insofar as existentialism analyzes human existence (as distinct from human potentiality), it analyzes human estrangement. Thus, in Tillich's approach existential analysis is one limited part of a total philosophy of life—the analysis of self-separation and estrangement.

In the *Systematic Theology* the life philosophies are understood to raise a third type of question—a question different from those raised by ontology or existentialism. The study of life reveals its deep ambiguity. All life is seen to be a mixture of creative and destructive processes; the very greatness of human life leads to its inevitable distortions. When life is viewed in all its tragedy, the question must be raised of an "unambiguous" life which is "beyond tragedy."[12] It is at this point that Christian theology and the philosophies of life can enter into fruitful dialogue. According to Tillich, the Christian concept of the divine Spirit can be presented as an answer to the ambiguities of life. Through the Spirit, man can be elevated into a unity with God's life which is eternal, beyond finite ambiguities.[13]

A fourth and final area of dialogue between philosophy and Christian theology must be mentioned. Men have perennially

---

[12]Tillich, *Systematic Theology*, III, p. 94.
[13]Cf. *ibid.*, Part IV, "Life and the Spirit."

pondered the possibility of meaning in human history. Christian thought has engaged, and must continue to engage, in debate with secular philosophies of history. Tillich does not, in fact, consider this area of investigation to be a separate part of the theological system; nor does he specify a school of philosophy with which he chooses to engage in dialogue. Rather, he interprets the question of meaning in history as a special subdivision of the quest for unambiguous life. He interprets history, therefore, in terms of the categories which he develops for the interpretation of life.

Just as man transcends himself in the vertical direction toward the infinite, so man in historical time moves beyond every finite moment, driving toward some final fulfillment. Life in the historical dimension never rests in any finite achievement; it "runs ahead toward the new."[14] It seeks that which is "absolutely new, symbolically expressed as 'New Creation.' "[15] Like all life, it is self-transcendent; it is finite but seeks the infinite. Since Tillich's view of life is "dialectical," this is true of his view of history also. This characteristic leads him to give special attention to the dialectical philosophies of history (the Hegelian and the Marxian views of history, for example).[16] According to Tillich, the Christian conception of the kingdom of God must be presented as a solution to the ambiguities of life in the historical dimension.[17]

We now have a basis for understanding the formal structure of Tillich's system of thought. Simply stated, it is a method of question and answer: the questions posed by philosophy, the answers provided by Christian theology. This form is followed in four major areas: the question of ultimate reality and the answer of God; the question of estrangement and the answer of reconciliation through the Christ; the question of the ambiguities of life and the answer of unambiguous life in the Spirit; and the question of meaning in history and the answer of the kingdom of God. These four dialogues are preceded by a discussion of the relation between reason as the instrument of philosophy and

[14]Cf. *ibid.*, p. 319.

[15]*Ibid.*, p. 326.

[16]Cf. *ibid.*, pp. 329-330.

[17]Cf. *ibid.*, Part V, "History and the Kingdom of God."

revelation as the source of religious insight. They are followed by a concluding discussion of the end and aim of life understood as participation in God's eternal life.

Tillich calls this approach to theology the "method of correlation"—the questions of philosophy are correlated with the answers of theology. Tillich proposes that if the method is to succeed, neither side can determine the content of the other. The philosophical question cannot prejudice the theological answer, and vice versa. They must be brought together in *form* so that they do, in fact, intersect; answers must answer questions, and questions must lead up to answers. This organization is the responsibility of the theologian, but he ought not to violate the autonomy of philosophy in so doing. When he investigates the material of philosophy, he *becomes* a philosopher.[18]

This method has fascinated the theological and philosophical worlds; both have attacked it vigorously. The attacks have, in part, cancelled each other. Some have held that Tillich's theological answers are determined by the way he formulates the philosophical questions.[19] Others, however, find evidence that Tillich's theology deeply affects the way in which the philosophical questions are formulated.[20] Our conclusion is that philosophy and theology deeply interpenetrate in Tillich's thought. This means that the simple formula of question and answer is misleading. Answer does, in part, shape question; question does, in part, affect answer. Nevertheless, there is genuine dialogue on a more profound level. Tillich is himself both philosopher and theologian; he grapples with the issues from both sides. His method is a useful way of taking account of both, although he never entirely abandons the one when he turns to the other.

No doubt it is true that Tillich enters into dialogue with some currents of modern philosophy and not with others. He was most deeply impressed by the dialectical philosophies of life which have their beginnings in Hegel, and he tended to press other

---

[18]Cf. especially Tillich, *Systematic Theology*, I, pp. 59-66.

[19]Cf. e.g., Hamilton, *op. cit.*

[20]Cf. e.g., Paul Ramsey, *Nine Modern Moralists* (Englewood Cliffs, N. J.: Prentice-Hall, Inc., 1962), pp. 181-196.

philosophies into this mold. But a recognition of his limitation in this respect need not blind us to what he accomplished.

Is Tillich's central insight concerning the nature of life philosophically or theologically derived? At first glance the idea of life as self-transcendence appears to be a purely philosophical notion, a complex theory of human self-consciousness. A more careful consideration reveals that Tillich's theory is a profound meditation upon the idea of resurrection. It is an elaborate explanation of the way in which God's power gains victory over death, the way in which the power of being resists nonbeing.[21] At this deepest level Tillich has fused the insights of philosophy and theology into an inseparable unity.

---

[21]Cf. Ramsey's suggestion to this effect in another context, *ibid.*, p. 184.

CHAPTER V

Revelation and God

TILLICH'S MAIN PURPOSE in writing the *Systematic Theology* is to give an account of the traditional Christian doctrines which will be compelling for modern man. Tillich takes classic Christianity seriously; he is not willing to see it dissolved into a vague religiosity. At the same time, he is inescapably a child of the modern age; in a period of unprecedented change in all areas of thought, he cannot simply repeat the religious formulae of the past. He must seek to express the insights of Christian faith in a vocabulary comprehensible and meaningful to modern man. Tillich cannot really speak to the man for whom "that ole-time religion is good enough"; nor will he finally convince the man for whom Christianity has no power. But for the one who must at once be Christian and modern man, Tillich's interpretations may have great relevance. The difficulty of his constructions ought not to deter such a one from coming to grips with his message.

We propose to have a look at Tillich's approach to five major Christian doctrines: God, man (sin and salvation), Christ, the church, and eschatology (last things). In these discussions we shall not be able to avoid the philosophical categories discussed in the preceding chapters, but we shall relate these ideas to the more traditional concepts. Our approach to this material will be unashamedly favorable. We shall look for that which seems to be genuinely helpful and constructive. Criticisms will largely be saved for a concluding section which will deal with problem areas in Tillich's thought.

Once again problems of method arise to plague us. We have discussed Tillich's use of philosophy and have indicated, in general terms, the type of insight which he derives from philosophical "reason." But if religion has some distinctive contribution (if it can answer philosophy's questions), what is the source of religious insight? What is meant by religious knowledge, and what is its relation to other ways of knowing? In an age dominated by the use of the scientific method as a reliable means of obtaining knowledge, the question of the source of religious insight becomes a vital one. Before we turn to Tillich's doctrinal contributions, we must examine his approach to the general question of religious knowledge.

Tillich's treatment of this area can best be dealt with in terms of the two concepts of ecstasy and revelation. Let us consider each of these in turn.

No doubt when one hears the word "ecstasy," he first thinks of some romantic experience, an ecstatic moment of happiness with one's beloved. Tillich is aware of this connotation, but he wants to salvage the word for a broader and deeper meaning which is still related to this more familiar usage. He suggests a return to the root meaning of the word: to stand outside of oneself. This meaning is present in the analogous expression that someone was "beside himself" (with exaltation, joy, grief, or the like). In Tillich's interpretation, ecstasy describes the condition in which some of the limitations of the structures of ordinary experience have been overcome. One stands beyond his own ordinary existence. Although the emotions may be involved in such an experience, it need not be predominantly emotional. As we shall see, it involves the intellect as well.

Tillich does agree with the popular view that genuine love is one example of ecstasy. Two human beings cannot be meaningfully united if each remains enclosed within himself. The ordinary structure of selfhood keeps us largely isolated from one another. Many cases of apparent unity in love are really various forms of disguised self-love; many others are based upon the sacrifice of the individuality and integrity of one of the partners. In Tillich's view true love, in which the individuality of the lovers is preserved, is possible only in God. One can get out of himself to be united with another only by being lifted above himself into a transcendent unity. All human beings are "at one" when they transcend their finite individualities in unity with the Divine; yet this is a kind of unity where individuality is maintained and affirmed. Other kinds of unity are destructive of full personhood.

To turn to the main theme of our discussion, the concept of ecstasy is significant in the area of religious knowledge. In Tillich's view the reception of revelation involves the ecstasy of reason. "Revelation" is the term usually employed to indicate the insight gained from some direct encounter with God. Judaism and Christianity (as well as Islam) are frequently identified as religions of revelation, which means that they originate from special encounters with God in which his will is revealed. Often revelation has been understood more specifically as supernaturally conveyed information about nature or about past or future historical events.

Tillich accepts the concept of revelation as an essential category for interpreting religious knowledge, but he rejects the idea of a body of supernaturally conveyed information. In his concise definition, "revelation is the manifestation of what concerns us ultimately."[1] In another expression, revelation appears when "the mind is grasped . . . , by the ground of being and meaning."[2] In the reception of revelation, the mind or reason is elevated beyond its normal structures; it is in a state of ecstasy in the sense discussed above. As far as reason is concerned, this means that God is not known in the ordinary forms of knowledge; he does not appear as an object to the thinking mind as a "subject." God does not appear as a thing in any sense: neither as an object of sight, nor as a literal voice, nor indeed as any kind of specific being. No finite content can be directly identified as divine.

It should be noted that Tillich interprets the concept of "miracle" in the context of the terms described here. He rejects the idea of miracle as an event which suspends the ordinary laws

---

[1]Tillich, *Systematic Theology*, I, p. 110.
[2]*Ibid.*, p. 112.

of nature. Admitting that the idea has taken on this connotation in modern usage, Tillich urges a return to an earlier and simpler meaning: namely, an occurrence which provokes astonishment and awe. Taken in this sense, miraculous event is inseparable from ecstatic response. Miracle and ecstasy both refer to an event in which there is a "manifestation of the mystery of being." Both terms describe an occurrence that is gripping, shocking, transforming, inspiring. These phenomena are aspects of the revelatory experience. Tillich would hold that those who knew Jesus experienced both. But the authentic experience of awe in the presence of mysterious power must be separated from the frequent expression of this experience in the form of legendary stories about Jesus' supernatural powers over nature.

What then is the real content of revelation, according to Tillich? The insight provided by revelation and gained in ecstasy falls into the general category of perspective upon facts already known. One's knowledge is illuminated and its inner meaning clarified by the discovery of its relationship to that which is ultimate. For example, in Tillich's view the Old Testament prophet was not given new information concerning Israel's political circumstances. Rather, he was enabled to discover the ultimate meaning of these circumstances through the ecstatic perspective. By the same token, Moses was not given a specifically new moral code, but was enabled to see the ultimate significance in a relative and conditioned morality. To Tillich revelation means being grasped by an ultimate within the relativities of time and space. In this approach many objects, events, and personal encounters can become revelatory; sacred documents, doctrines, and symbolic actions may preserve and mediate revelatory experiences. Actual revelation occurs when these finite things do mediate the divine Presence, when they do elicit a genuine ecstatic response. In Tillich's terminology all of these finite media of revelation become "symbols" for the divine Presence and his power; they mediate something which they do not themselves possess. We shall return to a discussion of symbols at a later point. It is important here to digest Tillich's point that revelation is characterized by the sense of ultimacy which it produces. Whatever provokes one's ultimate loyalty or grips one as an ultimate in meaning is revelation.

This "being grasped by an ultimate concern" in no way contradicts reason, for reason cannot cope with ultimates, whether in value, meaning, or being. It naturally seeks absolutes, but it finds them only ecstatically, in revelation, whereby it breaks through its ordinary structures. The conflict which arises is not between reason and revelation but between opposing revelations, or ultimate concerns. Many different ultimates have been passionately defended in human history. Can all of these be termed revelation? Tillich's answer would follow these lines: All of these ultimates are religious in character, and to the extent that ultimacy has been experienced, their proponents have been touched by the Divine. However, not all human religion can be evaluated favorably. Some of these ultimates have, in fact, mediated the divine Presence, but others have become demonic and idolatrous. Therefore, a criterion must be found to distinguish the true ultimate from false ultimates. Reason itself cannot serve this function; religion must be able to criticize itself.

Let us illustrate these points. A person in some situation of stress might affirm, "Nothing can deter me from telling the truth as I understand it." This person has been grasped by an ultimate commitment to the truth. Neither science nor philosophy can provide (or even explain) this form of experience; it is characteristically religious. It is a fragmentary revelation of the unconditional (or God); as such it is self-confirming to the person who receives it and can be challenged only from the standpoint of another ultimate concern. Such ultimates, however, may become idolatrous. If a person asserts, "This idea is absolutely true and cannot be criticized," absoluteness is attributed to something finite. Here ultimacy has again been sensed, but incorrectly received. True religion must consist of ultimacy received without an idolatrous response.

When we reach the question of the criterion or the norm by means of which revelation is judged, we arrive at the point where Tillich's doctrine of Christ becomes relevant. Tillich accepts the Christian affirmation that the revelation in Christ is normative, and provides a means for distinguishing true and false ultimates. We shall consider this problem in our discussion of Tillich's approach to the meaning of Christ. Let us at this point recapitulate what we have said about religious truth.

For Tillich, religion deals with ultimates or absolutes, with that which is unconditional. On the other hand, reason, whether in the form of philosophy or science, deals adequately only with the finite, the conditional, with that which is relative to time and place. Therefore, revelation and reason cannot conflict; they concern different dimensions of reality. In Tillich's view science is not concerned with ultimates at all, whereas philosophy asks the question of ultimates but cannot answer it properly. Thus, revelation has no relevance to science as such, but appears as the fulfillment of philosophical reason. The view of revelation as specific information must be rejected; it contradicts reason in both forms.

Revelatory insight is received in ecstasy in the sense that reason is beyond its normal structures. Just as in love the person is beyond himself without losing his integrity, so in revelation reason transcends itself without being destroyed. Any revelation which requires the sacrifice of reason is false. Revelation is something arresting, gripping, unavoidable; it comes to us rather than being our own creation. In the history of man the response to revelation has taken many forms: as ultimate commitment to a value or set of values; as ultimate devotion to a social, political, or religious cause; as ultimate confidence in a set of meanings found in existence; as ultimate security in the promise of resurrection. All of these ultimates are religious in quality, whether or not they belong to a formal religion. Many of them become idols and therefore play a destructive role in human life. The religious quality of these ultimates falsely received gives them a demonic power and influence. An ultimate received in an idolatrous manner can be combatted only by an ultimate properly received. In Tillich's belief, the New Testament picture of Jesus as the Christ manifests revelation properly grasped. (A note of warning must be registered here, lest we mislead the careful reader. Tillich maintains that religious experience is the medium, but not the content, of revelation. The significance of this may escape the general reader, but the student of religion will recognize its importance. Nineteenth-century liberal theology has been accused (and perhaps even convicted) of a preoccupation with the forms of human experience. Religious experience became the object of study rather than the God behind the experience. Thus Friedrich Schleiermacher (1768-1834) held that theology should study the modifications of the "feeling of absolute dependence." This, say twentieth-century theologians, is sheer subjectivism, man contemplating his own navel. Tillich seeks to avoid this charge by the above distinction between medium and content. It is not certain that he has succeeded, nor indeed is it perfectly clear that success is possible. Does science study the objects of our experience or our experience of objects? An answer would lead us into byways of the theory of knowledge which cannot be our concern here. Similarly we will note that Tillich is not subjectivistic by intention and then pass on discretely to less intractable issues.)

This is a helpful analysis of the distinctively religious quality of experience. Many of the conflicts of science and religion have arisen partly as the result of failure to make a distinction between that which carries ultimate significance and that which is recognized to be preliminary, finite, and relative. In some cases religion has erroneously claimed to have a special source of specific information; in others, science has taken upon itself an idolatrous sanctity and ultimacy. Both tendencies must be criticized as a form of getting out of bounds. When their proper limits are recognized, the two interests can live together peacefully.

Tillich's analysis also warns us against a too narrow conception of religious experience. American evangelicalism has rightly understood religious experience as something that takes hold of a person in a powerful way. However, this has been too narrowly understood as a certain type of emotional upheaval taking place in a religious setting. Tillich would not deny the authenticity of such an experience (although he would see certain dangers in it). Rather, he would view it as one culturally conditioned form of a more general phenomenon—the experience of being grasped by an ultimate concern. Having indicated that religion cannot be reduced to something else, we must now note that the reli-

62

gious can be a *quality* of anything else. The quality of ultimacy may appear in morality, in philosophical speculations, in art, even in science, as well as in institutional religion as such. Revelation may come through religious symbols, but it may also be mediated through other realms of human interest.

Tillich at once preserves the distinctiveness of religious insight and avoids confining it to a narrow segment of human experience. His terminology is cumbersome, but the basic issue is a vital one. Since the demise of revivalism, the American churches have tended to lose the sense of authenticity and compelling power. Tillich seeks to identify that which is compelling about religion, but in much broader and more liberal terms. The whole area identified with Tillich's terms *revelation* and *ecstasy* requires reexamination in our time, and Tillich has initiated some fruitful approaches to the problem.

From the question of religious knowledge we turn to the central doctrine in any theological system: the doctrine of God. Tillich's conception of God has been the most widely debated aspect of his system; yet some misunderstanding remains. We have already cited his initial definition: "God is being-itself." This definition has been the springboard for a great deal of criticism, centering in the argument that the concept of being-itself has no religious value. This criticism arises from the assumption that the concept of God as being-itself is lifeless, static, and impersonal. However, a closer inspection of Tillich's view casts the problem into a different perspective. As we have seen, Tillich understands being-itself in the sense of the power of being, the active negation of nonbeing. This is none other than the power of life to resist and to overcome the threat of death. The central symbol for God in Tillich's thought is "eternal life," the eternal power of being to affirm itself in the face of threat. The argument that Tillich's concept of being-itself is static and lifeless is thus without foundation.

The question of God as personal requires further consideration. We have noted that Tillich understands finite personhood in terms of self-transcendence and self-awareness (the subject-object relationship). Man becomes a self-conscious personal center by standing outside of himself in self-transcendence. This achievement is the realization of the greatest degree of individuality and separateness in the whole realm of being. We have also noted that Tillich attributes self-transcendence ("going out of himself") symbolically to God. Does this mean that we can speak (at least symbolically) of God as a self-conscious personal center? A positive answer would overlook Tillich's analysis of the relationship between eternal life and finite life. Let us consider this relationship.

We have spoken of finite potentialities as realities within the womb of the divine life. Actualization requires going out from this unity with the Divine. This separation is the basis for human freedom and self-consciousness. In Tillich's view, God's life goes out from itself in and through these finite existences. Thus God's self-transcendence is identical with man's; it is the same separation. Consider the following example: One may say that a mother's life, though in a sense fully realized, is also completed and fulfilled through the life of her child. Her final fulfillment comes when the child, after gaining independence, learns to love the mother in a mature way. The child's freedom is the mother's freedom also, at least in the sense that the mother freely allows the child's freedom. If we think of the whole process of going out and return (through love) as one complex life, we have an analogy for the relation between God and man in Tillich's theology. The analogy is limited in that the mother is already free, having previously been separated from *her* mother. We can conceive of an original source which goes out from itself only through its offspring. Its life is fulfilled through the life of the free offspring which return to it in love. This would seem to be a helpful analogy for the relation of God and man in Tillich's conception.

What conclusion, then, is reached concerning the issue of God as personal? Tillich's formal statement is as follows: "God is the ground of everything personal and . . . he carries within himself the ontological power of personality."[3] In a private dis-

---

[3]*Ibid.*, p. 245.

cussion Tillich used the expression that God "makes himself personal for personal being." Man must communicate with God in personal terms, for this is man's deepest level of communication. Man must pray to God as in personal address. But Tillich maintains that the sensitive religious person knows that he is not speaking to *a* person "out there"; God is already in the self and indeed in the prayer.[4] In the words of Paul: "For we do not know how to pray as we ought, but the Spirit himself intercedes for us with sighs too deep for words."[5]

Thus Tillich does not conceive of God as an individual personal center, a concept which, in his terms, would make God absolutely separate from everything else. Prayer to God cannot be construed as conversation between two personal centers. Rather, God is the ground and power of personhood which is actualized in finite persons. Again, he is the power of self-transcendence and freedom which is actualized in finite persons. In more technical language, God cannot be either subject (conscious mind) or object (thing); he is beyond the subject-object polarity. He cannot properly be conceived as *a* being, however great, or as *a* person, however supreme. God is the ground of both subject and object; he is beyond both.

Tillich holds that this view of God as the ground and power of being is implicit (though not always explicit) in the Scriptures, and that it came to be the normative view of classical Christian theology. He points out that in the early centuries the word "person" was applied to the three persons or "faces" of the Trinity, not to the unifying power of being which makes God divine. He argues that personalistic theism, in which God is described as a supernatural Person, did not appear within Christianity until the eighteenth century and should now once again be abandoned.

Tillich's critics, on the other hand, maintain that in this formulation Tillich has relapsed into pantheism. This is the view that God is to be equated with nature (at least the eternal aspects of nature), and it is a concept which has been con-

---

[4] *Ibid.*
[5] Romans 8:26.

sistently rejected by the church. Tillich answers that pantheism was rejected primarily because in equating God and nature, the possibility of human freedom was destroyed. In some pantheistic systems the individual existent becomes simply a "mode" of the eternal substance.[6] In Tillich's construction human freedom is the factor which "separates" the creation from the Creator. We have discussed Tillich's interpretation of freedom as self-transcendence. This movement of self-separation is also a separation from the divine ground, although it is achieved in the power of the divine life. It may be recalled that this "movement" is not spatial; we have suggested psychological separation between parent and child as an analogy with the ontological separation involved in the realization of freedom. Tillich, then, can be reconciled with a modified form of pantheism which preserves the authenticity of human freedom. The same may be said for certain modified forms of pantheistic naturalism. This means that one may begin by conceptualizing God as nature (as many pantheists have done), but a nature which contains the potentiality for human personhood, freedom, and rationality is quite different from a nature which is basically alien to these realities. Tillich is closer to pantheism than to the deistic concept of a divine Person, but he provides important correctives of the older forms of pantheism.

This reexamination of the Christian tradition with regard to the divine Being has great relevance in the context of the philosophical and theological currents of our time. It is a well-known fact that many modern philosophers from Nietzsche to Bertrand Russell and Jean-Paul Sartre have denied the reality of the God of theism. More recently, however, there has been evidence of a reconsideration of the problem within Christian thought itself. Perhaps the most widely discussed effort of this sort has been Bishop J. A. T. Robinson's popular essay, *Honest to God*. Robinson suggests that in order to face the realities of the modern world Christians must once and for all abandon the notion that God is in any sense "out there." He argues that Christians are too content to think in outworn categories in a

---

[6] Cf. Tillich's reference to Spinoza, *Systematic Theology*, I, pp. 237-238.

time when creative vision is required. It must be admitted that the effectiveness of Robinson's positive suggestions is diminished by the fact that he seeks to combine the insights of several contemporary theologians (including Tillich) without adequate recognition of their differences. However, his book provided a needed stimulus to further thought.

The debate concerning the proper conceptualization of the divine Being can be found also in the writings of a growing number of younger theologians in this country. These discussions have largely taken the form of responses to the enunciation of "the death of God" in the existentialist philosophy of Friedrich Nietzsche. These theologians, speaking from various perspectives, have all found some validity in Nietzsche's pronouncement. They raise questions concerning the intelligibility and the relevance of the concept of a supernatural person being. These thinkers do not propose to abandon the Christian perspective, but to reform-ulate it in contemporary terms.[7]

In the context of these radical reassessments Tillich's theology is at any rate not as startling as it seemed to be a decade ago. Indeed, the influence of Tillich is discernible in some aspects of these writings. Tillich has made it clear that in his view the protest of atheism against the existence of a divine Person is correct; no such Being can be discovered.[8] Furthermore, says Tillich, God does not "exist," if one uses the word "existence" properly. Existence characterizes finite beings which "stand out" from being-itself. The word God is a symbol for the infinite power of being which enables all beings to exist; but God is beyond existence and beyond the structures which give form to existence. He is the "abyss of being." This approach does not prevent Tillich from using symbolic words (such as "Father") to describe various aspects of our relationship to God. But these terms, though appropriate and valid, cannot be understood in their literal senses. (We shall return to the topic of symbolism later.)

Although to some Christians this idea of God may seem to be a radical departure from conventional thinking, it is actually

---

[7] Cf. Postscript to this volume.
[8] Tillich, *Systematic Theology*, I, p. 245.

rooted deeply in the Western philosophical and religious traditions. In addition, it is an approach which takes account of modern criticisms of personalistic theism; yet it would seem to preserve the essential elements of belief in God which one fears may be lost in the so-called "God is dead" theology.

This dual effectiveness is indicated by the fact that Tillich's theology has been severely criticized by both sides. The traditional theists argue that Tillich has lost all genuine transcendence in God and has merged God and nature in a pantheistic fashion. On the other hand, those theologians who have been influenced by positivism and the philosophy of linguistic analysis see in Tillich's thought a new effort to create an imaginary metaphysical world beyond the empirical world. They reject this construction as lacking any reliable means of verification.

Though each of these critiques has its point, it would appear that both miss the main thrust of Tillich's argument. One can approach Tillich's thought as an interpretation of two types of experience: the experience of the broken, tragic quality of finite human existence and the ecstatic experience of the holy which is "beyond tragedy." Tillich's interpretation of these experiences is that existence points beyond itself to that which precedes it and to that which consummates it. In Tillich's mode of expression this reality is directly "grasped"; religious experience is the medium through which this takes place. In his terms, reality is self-transcendent. But the whence and the whither of existence, toward which it points, is not a thing; "it" precedes the structures of the finite world which cast every entity into the form of subject or object. "It" is beyond the subject-object polarity. Faith's affirmation is that this whence and whither of existence is known because it becomes manifest fragmentarily within existence. There is only one reality; but this reality is self-transcendent. As a result of this self-separation, reality becomes self-contradictory and in need of reconciliation. Ultimately reconciliation is a self-reconciliation. Being is essentially one.

Thus Tillich has formulated a new approach to God's transcendence and immanence; in spite of criticism from both sides he has preserved both in a new combination. The point of contact between the Divine and the human is the experience of the holy or the ultimate—that which is beyond the subject-object relationship. The transcendence of tragic finitude which yet preserves the positive elements of finitude points toward that which is the ground and aim of existence. The self-transcending quality of finitude is the fundamental datum in Tillich's approach to God. God cannot therefore be equated either with nature (the realm of finite beings) or with any supernatural, objectively existing being; Tillich seeks rather to overcome the opposition between naturalism and supernaturalism. God is the power which drives finitude toward "in-finitude" and which fragmentarily lifts existence above this tragic quest into a reality where the conflict of finitude and infinity is overcome.

A word may be said specifically about Tillich's discussion of God at the end of *The Courage to Be*. In this often-quoted passage Tillich speaks of "the God above the God of theism."[9] He suggests that God as the power of being to affirm itself can still be known after faith in the God of theism has been dissolved in the acids of doubt and skepticism. The concept of God presented by Tillich in these pages is no different from the concept presented elsewhere in his writings. What appears to be exceptional here is the implication that all men have access to faith independently of revelation or the ecstatic reception of the holy. This has led some critics to speculate whether, in Tillich's view, the "absolute faith" described here can be detached from any and all historical traditions.

Two possible responses to this question may be derived from other parts of the system. First, Tillich holds that all men ask the question of God as a result of their finitude, which is threatened by nonbeing. The question itself presupposes an intuition of being-itself and truth-itself (not as *a* being, but as the object of ultimate concern). This intuitive knowledge of God is not normally viewed by Tillich as "saving" knowledge. It is the presupposition of the quest for God (both ontological and personal), and this quest terminates in ambiguity and tragedy (as we have seen in the systematic survey). Thus this knowledge would not seem to be an adequate source for the "courage to be."

[9] Tillich, *The Courage to Be*, pp. 182-190.

Secondly, Tillich maintains that there has been fragmentary revelation of God in all history. Reconciliation is partially realized in all of the religious traditions of the world. Thus all men would have access to some limited form of "saving" experience. In the section of *The Courage to Be* under consideration, Tillich speaks of a situation where all concrete religious symbols have been destroyed by doubt. He seems to say that whatever was powerful in these symbols can remain, although it is nameless and undefined. He further suggests that only the Christian church, with its message centering in the crucifixion, can point to the "God above the God of theism" and yet preserve its concrete symbols. This is true because Jesus displays absolute faith in spite of a sense of being forsaken by the God of theism. Tillich's reference to the crucifixion here seems to have two meanings: Jesus is presented as an example of absolute faith, and the Christian "symbol" of the crucifixion (the Christian interpretation of this event) contains the idea of a sacrifice of all human claims to certainty and assurance. According to Tillich, in the Christian view man is justified by faith not only in the face of moral guilt, but also in the face of intellectual doubt. In other words, it is not necessary to have the correct intellectual conception of God in order to share in the assurance of faith. The church which submits its own assurances to the cross can "mediate" a courage to be in the face of doubt and meaninglessness.

In summary, it seems clear that for Tillich absolute faith appears when symbols which once were meaningful lose their meaning. The power which once was mediated by these symbols continues to grasp the one for whom the symbols have lost their specific meaning. Thus revelation and ecstasy have taken place, although the symbols in which the revelation was expressed have lost their power. In this interpretation absolute faith is not entirely detached from a revelatory tradition. Tillich is attempting to speak to the man who experiences a deep anxiety over the loss of confidence in the symbols of his religious tradition. Tillich urges that the residual, courageous affirmation of life and the anxiety itself derive from a deeper faith which can be detached from the concrete symbols. This is not a stable or a desirable situation, but according to Tillich it is not an uncommon condition in our time.

Tillich shows here a commendable candor and sensitivity in seeking to approach those for whom the gradual erosion of faith has been a painful experience. The answer which he gives to the problem is provisional and temporary. In a broader perspective the question of a new and living symbolism must be raised. However, Tillich stands alone in contemporary theology in initiating such discussions. In so doing he has made a distinctive contribution.

CHAPTER VI

Man, Sin, and Salvation

WE NOW TURN to Tillich's analysis of human nature. Aspects of
Tillich's anthropology, or theory of man, are found in every
part of the system. In each part, problems posed by man's
existence are correlated with answers provided by the Christian
message. We have already surveyed Tillich's general approach to
man in our sketch of the systematic structure. Here we should
like to comment further upon Tillich's interpretation of sin as
estrangement and of salvation as reconciliation.

Many Christians would agree that the concept of sin has
become trivial in contemporary usage. The word is associated,
on the one hand, with old-fashioned revivalistic preaching of
hellfire and damnation and, on the other, with activities which
are somewhat more pleasurable by virtue of their "wickedness."
Sin has been identified with specific sins; the straightlaced
preacher is against them, but the man in the pew doubts that
they are all that bad.

Scholars and theologians have sought to restore the word "sin"
to its proper biblical meaning. In the Bible sin is fundamentally
rebellion against God and the consequent effort to place oneself (or some human creation) at the center of reality. Specific
sins (if they are truly such) are the outward manifestations or
symptoms of this primal sin. Sin can be overcome only through
reconciliation with God, not through moral effort alone.

The restoration of this biblical view of sin is much needed
and can be helpful. However, one might doubt that it provides
a complete solution to the problem. Some of the most potent
criticisms of Christianity (and Judaism) in the modern period

have centered around the accusation of "authoritarianism."
God, say these critics, is represented in the Bible as a patriarchal
tyrant, demanding unquestioning obedience. This image of God,
they suggest, is an archaism in modern life, a holdover either
from earlier stages in man's social evolution (Hegel and Marx)
or from the infant-father relationship (Freud). The concept of
sin, derived as it is from authoritarian religion, suggests a
servile obedience to an arbitrary despot. Modern man cannot
tolerate a moral law supposedly passed down from on high without rational justification. Man has the right to rebel against
such a conception of the divine rule. So runs the argument,
and many modern men recognize the force of it.

Tillich's formulation of the concept of sin is designed at once
to explicate the biblical view and to meet this modern attack
upon it. He first argues that the fundamental meaning of sin is
separation. Since the separation or alienation of man and God is
obviously a feature of the Old Testament account of Adam's
sin (either literally or mythologically interpreted), this assertion
is not surprising. One of the marks of sin is the erection of a
"dividing wall of hostility," in the Pauline phrase.[1] This separation, according to Tillich, can be described as "estrangement."
This term is not often used in the Bible, but the condition
which it describes is implicit in such stories as those of Cain and
Abel and of the tower of Babel, as well as in Paul's description
of man's fallen condition in the first chapter of Romans. The
Book of Job also reflects man's sense of estrangement from God.
The implications of the term "estrangement" lead Tillich to a
second observation. Estrangement means the separation of that
which was previously united; it assumes a prior unity. Thus, if
man has become estranged from God, he must have been previously united with God. Once again one may take the story
of Adam and Eve prior to the "fall" as an example. So far we
are quite certainly upon biblical grounds in our analysis.

It is in the further consideration of this original unity that
Tillich introduces certain new dimensions. He maintains that
that from which man is estranged must be in some sense "iden-

---

[1]Ephesians 2:14.

73

tical" with himself. All estrangement must finally be a "self-estrangement." Tillich reasons that the estrangement of two beings which are independent and self-contained cannot be of ultimate seriousness. The stronger the original unity, the more serious is the tragedy of separation. Thus the condition where "subject and object of the estrangement are identical" is the ultimate tragedy; reconciliation in this case is the "absolute demand."[2] Tillich concludes that the destructive aspects of human existence are derived from man's self-estrangement. It is this separation which constitutes sin; it is the overcoming of it which constitutes reconciliation. At the same time, however, he concludes that it is man's separation from God which leads to self-estrangement.

Tillich's analysis at this point is derived from the systematic structure which we surveyed earlier. Man's life in its initial potentiality or essence is "within" God; it is finite but in continual unity with the power of being. This condition of humanity in continual unity with the power of being constitutes man's essence (what man is potentially and ought to be in fact). The one thing missing from full manhood is freedom. The realization of freedom, however, involves a movement "outside" of the divine life into finite separation. In this movement man becomes estranged from his potential being, from his essential unity with the power of being, from his life within God. Estrangement is necessary in order to actualize freedom and self-transcendence. Reconciliation might be conceived as a return to the womb of the Divine, but this would be the destruction of freedom. The only other form of reconciliation would be the entrance of divine power into estranged existence. Christianity affirms that this is exactly what has taken place in the events centering around the person of Jesus of Nazareth. Through this act of divine grace, the realization of man's original nature within free but estranged existence is achieved. What was first realized in Christ is made available to all men, at least fragmentarily, through the divine Spirit. We have indicated in our discussion of ecstasy what

---

[2]Tillich, "Estrangement and Reconciliation in Modern Thought," *Review of Religion*, IX (November, 1944), p. 6. This understanding of estrangement is implicit throughout the *Systematic Theology*.

Tillich means by the appearance of the Divine or the ultimate within existence. Through this appearance self-estrangement and estrangement from God are overcome.

If sin is separation from and contradiction of one's true nature, and if salvation is the realization of that nature through reunion, then the charge that Christianity is authoritarian is groundless. Sin means self-disruption; disobedience to God's law means rebellion against one's own proper fulfillment. It is man's true nature to be in unity with God; in separation from God his life begins to disintegrate. Reconciliation with God is at the same time self-reconciliation. Thus, Tillich combines the religious concern for union with God with the humanistic concern for self-realization.

Involved in this approach is Tillich's acceptance of the idea of a universal "fall" (or estrangement) of man. This traditional concept, usually associated with the story of Adam and Eve, has been largely disregarded by liberal Christianity. In liberal thought, something that happened to a first man, even if true, could not have any relevance many centuries and eons later. In Tillich's view the story of Adam and Eve is symbolic of the estrangement of man—of all men—from the ground of his being. The blissful and innocent state in the garden of Eden represents for Tillich the condition of pure potentiality within the divine life. The act of disobedience is symbolic of the separation which occurs through the assertion of freedom and independence. Accompanying the realization of freedom is the appearance of self-awareness ("they knew that they were naked"). The realization of freedom and self-awareness is a positive step, but it is paralleled by the appearance of a sense of guilt and the fear of death. To Tillich this story is the classic mythological description of man's universal estrangement.[3]

Tillich's position on this matter includes the view that all men inevitably fall into sin in the process of becoming fully human. This means further that man cannot eliminate sin or estrangement and become reconciled through his own moral efforts. Thus Tillich raises again the traditional issue of pre-

---

[3]Cf. Tillich, *Systematic Theology,* II, pp. 29-44.

destination versus free will, and he clearly takes the side of predestination in his view that man cannot initiate his own salvation. Once again, American religious thought has tended to abandon the thought framework of Calvinism with its emphasis upon predestination. The tone of American life has been activist and moralistic; religiously speaking, man must be free to "work out his own salvation." In this respect the Protestant churches have lost the central insights of the Protestant Reformation, insights which Tillich seeks to recapture.

Tillich tries to reinstate the view that in the relationship between God and man, God is always active, and man is the recipient of God's reconciling activity. Tillich views this principle as the very heart of Protestantism, as the theme from classical Protestant thought (in Luther and Calvin) which is most relevant for man today. "It should be regarded as the Protestant principle that, in relation to God, God alone can act and that no human claim, especially no religious claim, no intellectual or moral or devotional 'work,' can reunite us with him."[4] There are several implications of this position which should be examined.

The initial assumption is the point already made that estrangement is universal. This means that no human action can be reconciling in an unambiguous way. Our best efforts to overcome separation and to achieve the good contain the seeds of further estrangement. If we are to be reunited with God (and with our best natures), God must take the initiative. From this conclusion certain limitations of human capabilities follow. Man must recognize that no acts of religious piety can purify him; no moral effort can make him righteous. Tillich adds a third disclaimer which he thinks has been implicit, though not explicit, in the Protestant position: No act of believing specific doctrines can place man securely within the truth of God. This position, in sum, is the meaning of Luther's doctrine of "justification by grace through faith."[5]

---

[4] Tillich, *Systematic Theology*, III, p. 224. Used by permission.
[5] Cf. *ibid.*

Tillich holds that Luther's doctrine requires reinterpretation in order to clarify its relevance for modern man. Men in the contemporary period are not typically aware of a need to be justified in the eyes of God. They do not have, as Luther had, a strong sense of God's wrathful condemnation. However, modern men do have, according to Tillich, a strong need to be "accepted." It is not always clear by whom we desire to be accepted (society? ourselves? God?), but many of our thoughts and actions are attempts to justify ourselves and to prove ourselves acceptable. For many people this attempt becomes life's major preoccupation. In this context Tillich argues that the doctrine of justification by grace through faith can be meaningfully translated. Its essential meaning is the assertion that "we are accepted by God although being unacceptable according to the criteria of the law (our essential being put against us) and that we are asked to accept this acceptance."[6] The "good news" of the Christian message is "that, although unacceptable, I am accepted."[7]

The act of faith, then, in Tillich's construction is the act of "accepting my acceptance" in spite of my awareness that I am not worthy of acceptance. In agreement with the Reformers, Tillich holds that even the act of faith is the result of grace—it is "the state of being grasped by the Spiritual Presence."[8] In Tillich's view the idea that faith is a human work is the last bastion of those who seek self-salvation; even here it must be affirmed that in the relation of God and man, God is active, and man is the recipient of God's action. This is Tillich's interpretation of the words of Paul: "For by grace you have been saved through faith; and this is not your own doing, it is the gift of God—not because of works, lest any man should boast."[9]

Although the theme of justification by grace through faith was the rallying point of classic Protestantism, the Protestant movement in its diversity has not often remained loyal to it, and its application has become problematical in the modern period.

---

[6]*Ibid.*, pp. 224-225.
[7]*Ibid.*, p. 222.
[8]*Ibid.*, p. 221.
[9]Ephesians 2:8-9.

Tillich feels, however, that the principle, when expressed in contemporary terminology, is discovered to be an insight of great psychological profundity. We might attempt to illustrate its application. In a certain type of family a child may be given to understand (either verbally or in less conscious ways) that he will not be accepted and loved by the parents until he obeys their commands. When he disobeys, he is rejected; he becomes unacceptable. This child may decide that he cannot often please his parents. Yet when he fails, that which he wants most, their love and acceptance, is withheld from him. He therefore becomes rebellious and in despair rejects their commands altogether.

Another family may project a deep sense of loving acceptance of a child. He knows that he is accepted in spite of unacceptable actions. This child, in the long run, will be more successful in pleasing his parents than the first. He is basically at one with them through love in spite of the ups and downs of his behavior. Tillich seems to say that something like this must be true of the relation between God and man. If man is secure in his relationship to God, he is able to approximate more fully the fulfillment of his best nature as God desires.

In Tillich's approach the moral law which judges man is the law of his own essential nature. To be united with God (at least fragmentarily) in the relationship of faith is to fulfill (at least partially) what the law requires. Thus, to this extent man is free from the law; he lives "in the Spirit," in the Pauline expression. Furthermore, in Tillich's account the man who is justified through faith is free from specific moral commands which are relative and may become outmoded and oppressive. Unity with God in the Spirit is above all moral laws. This "freedom of the Christian man" (Luther's phrase) requires great maturity and can never be complete. Estrangement and the need for moral commandments remain. Nevertheless, in an age of moral uncertainty like our own, when traditional moral standards are being challenged, there is great need for the Christian perspective of life in the Spirit. Tillich's formulation of the problem of faith and works is a relevant restatement of these insights of the Reformation.

The doctrine of justification by grace through faith has another application in Tillich's thought. As we have seen, he understands the principle to involve a rejection of all forms of self-salvation. In his view there is a trend toward this effort in all religions, and the "Protestant principle" is a necessary safeguard against it. One central aspect of the effort of man to save himself is his inclination to make something finite and human into an absolute. This may take the form of making absolute a certain form of human virtue (hence, self-righteousness); it may involve the elevation of doctrinal beliefs into the status of absolute truth (hence, dogmatism). It may appear as the claim of infallibility of the church (as in Roman Catholicism) or of the words of the Bible (as in Protestant fundamentalism). In the secular realm it may appear as the sanctification of the nation or race. Wherever men construct their own finite absolutes, the Protestant "protest" is appropriate; only God is God, and no finite reality can provide God's salvation. As Tillich expresses it: "The Protestant principle . . . contains the divine and human protest against any absolute claim made for a relative reality, even if this claim is made by a Protestant church."[10] Thus, the Protestant principle provides the basis for detecting and rejecting all idolatry.

A legitimate question may be raised at this point. If reconciliation is by God's grace, if faith is a gift of God, is there nothing a man can do to seek reconciliation? If nothing can be done, are all human interest and concern futile? Tillich's answer to this question is so direct that his own words must be quoted in full:

If, however, the question—What can I do in order to experience the New Being?—is asked with existential seriousness, the anwer is implied in the question, for existential seriousness is evidence of the impact of the Spiritual Presence upon an individual. He who is ultimately concerned about his state of estrangement and about the possibility of reunion with the ground and aim of his being is already in the grip of the Spiritual Presence.[11]

---

[10]Tillich, *The Protestant Era*, p. 163.
[11]Tillich, *Systematic Theology*, III, p. 223. Used by permission.

The answer, then, is implicit in the question. He who seeks reconciliation and his true being with passionate commitment has already been grasped by the grace which creates faith.

This theme in Tillich must be associated with his conviction that God's reconciling grace appears fragmentarily in all human history and in all religions. Tillich is willing to partition both revelation and salvation; both appear partially in all times and all places. Though, as we shall see, he affirms the centrality and normativeness of the revelation in Christ, he sees the possibility of a positive relationship among the world's religions.

It is obvious that the theme of justification by grace through faith has played a central role in the formation of Tillich's theological system. At the risk of excessive quotation we must document this influence with his own testimony. Concerning his personal appropriation of this Protestant principle, Tillich writes:

You cannot reach God by the work of right thinking or by a sacrifice of the intellect or by a submission to strange authorities, such as the doctrines of the church and the Bible. You cannot, and you are not even asked to try it. Neither works of piety nor works of morality nor works of the intellect establish unity with God. They follow from this unity, but they do not make it. They even prevent it if you try to reach it through them. But just as you are justified as a *sinner* (though unjust, you are just), so in the status of *doubt* you are in the status of truth. And if all this comes together and you are desperate about the meaning of life, the seriousness of your despair is the expression of the meaning in which you still are living. This unconditional seriousness is the expression of the presence of the divine in the experience of utter separation from it. It is this radical and universal interpretation of the doctrine of justification through faith which has made me a conscious Protestant.[12]

One can only admire the combination of intellectual honesty and religious passion reflected in this passage. It is this fusion of radical intellectual integrity and deep commitment which makes Tillich a most effective spokesman for modern Christianity.

Tillich's approach to sin and salvation is in some respects more pessimistic, and in other respects more optimistic, than the conventional views with which most people are familiar. On the

---

[12]Tillich, *The Protestant Era*, Author's Introduction, p. xv. Used by permission.

one hand, Tillich's emphasis on the universal fall of man leads him to the view that human life is tragic; evil pervades the highest achievements of which we are capable. At the same time, in his view, unlike most traditional views, there is a positive aspect to the fall of man—the realization of freedom and self-awareness. The fall is not unambiguously evil. Indeed, it is tragic in the sense of combining good and evil. Again, on the one hand Tillich holds that man can achieve no reconciliation apart from God's grace; yet he sees grace as a pervasive power in human life and human history. God's reconciling activity is not solely confined to one point in time.

Tillich's discussion of these topics is an important reconsideration of familiar themes. He is fully aware of the strengths of the Christian tradition in interpreting human existence. At the same time he takes account of the insights of modern psychology and of the criticisms brought to bear against Christian thought in modern philosophy.

CHAPTER VII

The Doctrine of Christ

OUR FOURTH MAJOR AREA of interest is the doctrine of Christ, or Christology. The traditional Christian understanding of the person of Christ was given formal expression at the Council of Chalcedon in the fifth century A.D. The Chalcedonian creed affirms that in Jesus the Christ two natures (divinity and humanity) were united in one person without loss of the distinctive characteristics appropriate to each. This formulation has been traditionally associated with the statement in John's Gospel that the divine Word which was with God from the beginning "became flesh and dwelt among us."[1] Employing the Chalcedonian formula as an interpretation of John's meaning, we arrive at the doctrine of the incarnation: In Jesus the divine Word assumed human nature. Throughout the history of the church this doctrine has been much debated, and a variety of approaches to it have been proposed. In modern times the idea of a historical incarnation of the Divine has been both sharply attacked and vigorously defended. Most Christians agree that some reformulation is needed. However, some feel that the Chalcedonian formula sets the indispensable basis for all discussions, while others seek a more thoroughgoing revision.

Although Tillich explicitly seeks a path between orthodoxy and liberalism,[2] his approach belongs, no doubt, on the more liberal side of the debate. Nevertheless, he takes full account of the major issues raised in past controversies. Through an impres-

---

[1] John 1:14.
[2] Cf. Tillich, *Systematic Theology*, II, p. 150.

sive reconsideration of the entire tradition he reaches a fresh expression of the doctrine which, he believes, still preserves the content essential to the historic Christian witness.

He first urges that great caution must be employed in the use of the word "incarnation." As an expression of the "paradox that he who transcends the universe appears in it," the term has a legitimate meaning.[3] But insofar as it suggests a transmutation of the Divine into the human, its meaning is not only mythological but is a misleading symbol which must be rejected. The same may be said for the expression, "the Word became flesh." According to Tillich, the Divine is and remains divine; it cannot become something else. In a critique of Tillich's position George H. Tavard points out that in the traditional view the Word retains its divinity when it assumes human nature.[4] This observation, however, does not remove the point that in traditional Christian imagery the Word goes through some transformation in assuming flesh. If it remains entirely unchanged, the word incarnation would lose its meaning. For example, the term incarnation surely seems to suggest that the Divine became localized in time and place. Tillich seeks to express more effectively the paradox that that which is inherently beyond time and place was *manifested in* time and place. He holds that the word incarnation does not preserve this distinction adequately.

Secondly, Tillich (at this point in agreement with a number of contemporary theologians) suggests the abandonment of the "two natures" vocabulary. This suggests two realities "which lie beside each other like blocks and whose unity cannot be understood at all."[5] Tillich calls for a formulation which expresses the relation in more dynamic terms. Here his position becomes more distinctively his own. For him a dynamic view requires that the unity of the divine and the human natures in Christ not be simply a juxtaposition of two fundamentally distinct and alien natures. The unity must be "essential": that is, in accord with the original (or eternal) structures of humanity and divin-

---

[3]*Ibid.*, p. 149.
[4]Cf. Tavard, *Paul Tillich and the Christian Message*, pp. 121-124.
[5]Tillich, *Systematic Theology*, II, p. 148.

ity. The unity cannot be an arbitrary fusion of radically opposing realities; it must be the reestablishment of a "prior" or eternal unity.

These considerations lead Tillich to reinterpret the traditional doctrine of the incarnation as the historical realization of "eternal God-man-unity" or "Eternal God-Manhood."[6] As we have seen, Tillich considers man's "original" or "essential" nature to be an already partially individualized potentiality within the divine life. In this state prior to actual existence man is finite, but the threats of finitude are continually overcome through man's unity with the power of being. The only aspect of man lacking in this state is actualized freedom. As we have indicated, the unity of man with the power of being is lost in the actualization of freedom. In the person of Christ, however, the estrangement is overcome, and the original and essential unity is reestablished. Furthermore, this is accomplished in actual existence (which includes freedom), not in the form of a return to the womb of the Divine. Tillich calls this the "essentialization" of existence or the realization of the "New Being" (following Paul's concept of the "new creation").[7] In Tillich's understanding the New Being does not consist simply of a return to the starting point, to essence. The new creation includes that which is positive in existence, namely, freedom and that which is built upon freedom. In Christ, then, the fulfillment of human life is realized, and the reconciliation of essence and existence is achieved. Christ is what man potentially is and ought to be.

When the question is asked why this should be achieved in Jesus and not in some other, Tillich again suggests a reconsideration of the tradition. Emphasis has traditionally been placed upon the argument that the incarnation was foreordained by God from the beginning. Tillich maintains that this is a one-sided answer to the question, an answer which does not take the humanity of Jesus with full seriousness. In his view one of the basic structures of all life is the "polarity," the dynamic interaction, of destiny and freedom, neither one of which is comprehensible

---

[6]*Ibid.*
[7]Galatians 6:15.

without the other. The free decisions of an individual stem from his character, his centered self. The self is shaped by the individual's response to the totality of the world's impact upon him. His character is inescapable; it is his destiny. Nevertheless, in self-transcendence the self stands beyond itself; it is not confined within itself; it is free. This freedom is limited, but not eliminated, by the destiny of the self. Similarly, destiny must be qualified by freedom; it is open to the future.

Tillich is uncompromising in applying this polarity to the life of Jesus. On the side of destiny it is appropriate to speak of the coming of Jesus "at the right time."[8] His life and mission cannot be understood except in the context of the whole history of his people; the impact of the Christian movement depended in part upon the receptivity of the Graeco-Roman environment into which his early followers moved. According to Tillich, Christians correctly see God's providence or predestining in the realization of the New Being here and not elsewhere. History was moving in this direction.

Nevertheless, Tillich maintains that it was necessary for Jesus to affirm his destiny in freedom. Like all other men, Jesus could reject his mission; were this not the case, it would be meaningless to say that he was tempted to do so. Freedom involves "tensions, risks, dangers." With this consideration in mind Tillich urges the propriety of a Christology of "adoption" to balance the Christology of incarnation.[9] Jesus did not become the revealer of God until he affirmed his destiny to be the Christ in finite freedom. One cannot, of course, identify a moment when he did so decisively. Tillich appears to hold that throughout Jesus' life he maintained an unbroken unity with the Father. This would mean that in all of his free acts he affirmed his mission as bearer of the New Being. But Tillich accepts as a needed corrective the view that Jesus was "adopted" by God on the basis of the quality of his life in freedom. This is one side of the picture, but to Tillich it is essential to the preservation of Jesus' humanity. Adoptionism seems implicit in several New Testament passages (for

---

[8]Romans 5:6.
[9]Tillich, *Systematic Theology*, II, p. 149.

example, the account of Jesus' baptism), but it was rejected by the early church. Tillich's dialectical view of man enables him to hold this theme in polarity with incarnation, and thus he is able to deal more adequately with the humanity of Jesus.

What, then, is accomplished by the appearance of the New Being in Jesus? It is perhaps correct to say that Tillich puts his emphasis upon the fulfillment of "revelation" in Christ, but it is important to understand what he means by this term. In the more literalistic branches of Christianity (from which American Christianity largely descends), revelation has been understood as a supernatural communication of information about divine things. Revelation understood in this way conveys knowledge about God's laws for man, about God's intentions for the future, or about the divine nature itself. The recipient of the revelation and those who are later told about it are free to act or not to act on the basis of this information. Revelation does not of itself effect any change in the character of the recipient, according to this view. Revelation in this sense may be preserved for posterity in a book or in a body of doctrines. It becomes the content of faith, the *depositum fidei,* originally supplied by God, but now detached from God and put into the keeping of human beings.

Tillich categorically rejects this view of revelation. On the contrary, for him the effect of revelation is to bring the believer into the actual presence of God. Expressed differently, revelation is the ecstatic experience of the presence of the holy. This view is reflected in Tillich's assertion that revelation and salvation are not to be separated. Revelation is not available to the detached or disinterested observer; it is present only for him who is drawn into the revelatory context and receives its transforming impact. This is not to say that revelation is always totally realized or totally absent; both revelation and salvation may be fragmentary. Here Tillich adopts a liberal position: He sees fragmentary revelation and salvation in all historical eras and in all human cultures. But he understands the central Christian affirmation to be the claim that the revelation in Christ is the fulfillment of and the criterion for all revelation. For the Christian, revelation in Christ is final in the sense that it cannot be surpassed or replaced; it is itself the standard by which any other claim of revelation must be judged.

In what way, then, did Jesus bring men into the presence of God? In Tillich's expression he was "transparent to . . . , the divine mystery."[10] Expressed differently, Jesus displays what a human life is like which preserves a continuous unity with the transcendent ground and source. Thus he manifests God to man and at the same time reveals the nature of true humanity. In Tillich's view this transparency could be achieved only by one who was willing to sacrifice all that was finite in himself to that which was divine. Thus all that was finite in Jesus had to be given up in order that the Christ might be manifest in him. That which was finite in Jesus was relative and historically conditioned; he could manifest the eternal only by surrendering the temporal. Lest this seem entirely negative, it must be noted that one can willingly surrender only that which he fully possesses. The capacity of willing self-sacrifice for a transcendent purpose is a mark of courage and strength, not of weakness.

In Tillich's view the cross of Christ is the most powerful symbol for the presence of God. A symbol for Tillich is a finite reality which actually mediates the presence of the Divine. Thus the crucifixion, as itself a representation of the entire sacrificial life of Jesus, is for Christians the central revelatory event of history. This assertion is made on the basis of "daring faith" rather than rational certainty. At the same time Tillich draws from this assertion (as well as from rational considerations) a characteristic of an effective symbol for God: It must contain the negation of its own finitude. We shall examine Tillich's concept of symbol closely in a later section.

This discussion of the person of Jesus raises the question of the authenticity of the historical records. Can we be sure that Jesus actually existed as he is portrayed in the Gospels? It is clear that the efforts of several generations of biblical scholars to get behind the Gospels to the "historical Jesus" made a deep impression upon Tillich's mind. After a careful consideration

---

[10]Tillich, *Systematic Theology*, I, p. 135. Tillich elsewhere suggests that "translucent" is a better term, indicating the effect of the medium upon that which is transmitted.

of the results of such research Tillich concluded that the "quest for the historical Jesus" (Albert Schweitzer's phrase) inevitably fails. It is not possible to get behind the Gospels to the "real" Jesus. The only Jesus we have is the Jesus of the Gospels; the only Christ to be found is "the New Testament picture of Jesus as the Christ." This is at once a chastening and a liberating conclusion. It is chastening in that we cannot get behind the reception of Jesus to the way he really was, independent of all reactions to him; it is liberating in that we know for certain how he was received and need not wait for the latest results of biblical scholarship.

Jesus was received by the members of the New Testament community as the Christ, the bearer of the New Being. In their ecstatic experience God had been manifested in their midst, and a reconciliation had been achieved. Later generations of those standing in this tradition have found that the New Testament picture of Jesus as the Christ mediates God's presence to them also. Thus, in Tillich's view revelation is self-authenticating. This does not mean that all of the historical details of the gospel record are necessarily correct. The writers of the Gospels sought various modes of expression to indicate in concepts available to them the impact of Jesus' life upon them. Some of these modes of expression are mythological or legendary. The ecstatic experience of the holy cannot, after all, be properly described in literal terms. But the main intention of the gospel records is to express the conviction that in Jesus a new eon has been inaugurated, a new possibility for human life has been initiated. This claim is also the faith of the church, in spite of the fallibility of the historical records.

This approach to the New Testament deals honestly with the problems of cultural relativity and the fallibility of the records. Tillich urges that the Christian tendency to absolutize these writings is a mistaken impulse. It is seeking the unconditioned where it cannot be found—in the limited and historically conditioned response to revelation. However, this response preserved in the Scriptures can become the *medium* of revelation for those who are receptive to its central message. The only absolute is the actual presence of the Divine, received in a revelatory experience. For Christians the revelation received in the event of Christ is primary; all others are secondary and derivative. This conviction is admittedly a decision of faith, but according to Tillich all commitment to ultimates is a matter of faith. The choice of an "ultimate concern" always involves risk and individual decision.

This approach to the person of Christ and to the records concerning him seems to this writer to suggest in broad outlines the constructive yet critical approach required by modern Christians. In spite of certain limitations which will be considered later, Tillich's formulation seems to embody the strengths of Christian liberalism while avoiding its weaknesses.

Two different reactions to Tillich's Christology from careful scholars may be noted. Father George H. Tavard, in a full-length study of Tillich centering upon his doctrine of Christ, concludes that in forsaking the Chalcedonian formula Tillich falls into "heterodoxy," and his approach is therefore unacceptable. In revising the traditional doctrine Tillich has lost "both the Christ-character and the Jesus-character of Jesus the Christ."[11] His reformulation can only be viewed as seriously deficient from the standpoint of Christian orthodoxy. Tavard reaches this conclusion in spite of his admiration for Tillich's profundity and penetration.

On the other hand, Bernard Martin, a Jewish scholar, has suggested that modern Christians should be thankful that Tillich has made the doctrine of Christ "at least comprehensible."[12] Though Martin ventures no opinion about Tillich's accord with the traditional view, and though Martin is not himself committed in faith to it, he feels that he can appreciate Tillich's approach to Christ as possibly meaningful and relevant for modern man. These contrasting views point up the problem for the modern Christian. If he seeks always to preserve and defend Christian orthodoxy, he may rephrase his faith to gain freshness of style, but he can never allow criticism to affect the inner structure of

---

[11]Tavard, *Paul Tillich and the Christian Message,* p. 132.
[12]Martin, *op cit.,* p. 179.

his belief. This Christian wards off the blows of modern thought but never enters into creative dialogue with it. Another may find, however, that he is at once a modern man and a Christian. He cannot abandon either standpoint; he must, for the sake of his own mental well-being, bring them into some form of unity. It is to this latter man that Tillich speaks most forcefully. Tillich also is at once a child of modern life and a Christian. He must, and he does, bring the two perspectives into productive relationship. For many Tillich exemplifies the true function of Christian theology.

CHAPTER VIII

Man in the Social Dimension

IN A SYSTEMATIC SURVEY of Christian doctrine, the fourth major doctrinal area is usually referred to as the doctrine of the church. In considering Tillich's approach to the church, however, we must deal also with his general analysis of human culture. We must, in other words, consider the social dimension of man's existence in its totality. This requires a study of culture and church individually and in interaction. This whole discussion takes its point of departure from Tillich's conviction that religion is essentially social. He asserts that "the divine Spirit's invasion of the human spirit does not occur in isolated individuals but in social groups."[1] This emphasis is a needed corrective to American individualism in religion.

When we turn to Tillich's analysis of the social dimension of man's existence, three central concepts appear which require identification. Two of these are readily identifiable. First, the word "culture" describes the general, observable pattern of life of a particular social group at a particular time. Second, the institutional church is the observable social organization which embodies the Christian movement in its various branches. The third concept describes a less observable reality. Tillich coins the term "Spiritual Community" to describe the new social reality which is the result of the impact of divine revelation. It is the social correlate of the New Being; it cannot be identified with any particular social institution.

---

[1] Tillich, *Systematic Theology*, III, p. 139.

Tillich holds that wherever men are grasped by the divine Presence, there Spiritual Community is created. This occurs fragmentarily in all human cultures and in all periods of history. It is found within religious institutions, but also apart from them in supposedly secular groups. Even groups which are explicitly antireligious may be its representative in specific contexts. How, then, is this kind of community to be recognized? Clearly some norm is required which would provide criteria for its identification. The Christian affirms that this norm is found in the Spiritual Community formed in response to the revelation through Jesus as the Christ. Tillich suggests five such criteria (using the New Testament story of Pentecost as his general model).[2] First, the presence of the Divine, or the Holy, is received ecstatically (in the sense defined earlier). Second, the members of the group form a community of faith in the sense that they are grasped by a common "ultimate concern." Third, it is a community of love. Tillich recognizes that there are many varieties of the love relationship, but in Spiritual Community these must be to some degree influenced by *agape* or "self-surrendering love." Fourth, the community must establish a unity which transcends individual, as well as national, cultural, and racial differences. Finally, it must seek universality; by its very nature Spiritual Community seeks to include all mankind. Wherever these marks are present, even fragmentarily, there Spiritual Community may be discerned. (No doubt Tillich would encourage debate as to whether other marks might be included.)

To distinguish between those communities which result from the impact of normative revelation (the revelation through Christ) and those which have other sources, Tillich speaks of "manifest" and "latent" Spiritual Community. The latter either has no access to the central revelation, or it explicitly rejects this revelation. Nevertheless, the quality of its life indicates its source in some "Spiritual Presence." The crucial difference between the two types is that manifest Spiritual Community possesses within itself a final criterion of self-criticism. All religious communities are subject to demonic distortions (as we shall see in our discus-

---

[2]Cf. *ibid.*, pp. 151-157.

sion of the churches). Communities based upon the revelation in Christ can "actualize a radical self-negation and self-transformation as it is present in reality and symbol in the Cross of Christ."[3] This mark of the Christian churches is the "Protestant principle," which we have already discussed.

One further characteristic of Spiritual Community is that in it there is no special religious function. In this kind of group, religion and "way of life" are one. Every cultural expression is aware of its own religious depth. Of this kind of society it can be said: "Religion is the substance of culture, culture is the expression of religion."[4] Similarly, there is no separation between religion and morality. In Spiritual Community that which is demanded by the moral law is done through grace and therefore without compulsion. Here one does by natural inclination what the law requires. There is no contrast between the sacred and the secular, no conflict between moral self-reliance and religious receptivity. This kind of society, needless to say, is never found in its pure form.

Now we must relate Spiritual Community to actual human cultures, on the one hand, and to the actual churches on the other. Spiritual Community is hidden; it cannot be identified with any social institution; it transcends national and cultural boundaries. At the same time it cannot be fully understood apart from an understanding of Tillich's approach to culture and church. We shall look at each of these in turn.

Man is creative, and that which he creates is "culture," in Tillich's sense of the word. Included in the scope of this concept (which may be rendered loosely as "civilization") are all material products and modes of production, all social institutions, all patterns of thinking and acting, all artistic creations. Tillich understands all of the products of human culture to be aspects of man's self-creation, which is one of the basic functions of life. In all creativity there is an element of self-transcendence, as we have seen. Since self-transcendence is a striving for the infinite, there is a hidden religion in all culture, even in those cultures

---

[3] *Ibid.*, p. 154.
[4] Tillich, *The Protestant Era,* Author's Introduction, p. xvii.

which deny religion. From the standpoint of his general analysis of life Tillich thinks that it is possible to identify three different types of culture in terms of their general tone and quality. Each type of culture adopts a distinctive attitude toward the question of ultimate reality.

The first type of culture (first in the sense of original and also final) Tillich terms "theonomy." A theonomous culture is one in which all cultural creations reflect a sense of their grounding in the eternal. This can be true not only of painting and sculpture, of literature and music, but also of social patterns of behavior, philosophical theories, political structures, even technical tools. No cultural concern is viewed as *purely* preliminary and relative; all are rooted in an ultimate concern, and all have an ultimate significance. The example usually given by Tillich of such a culture is the period of early and high Middle Ages in the Western world. One can see this religious quality in the painting, architecture, philosophy, political theory, and morality of the period. However, the concept applies more broadly to the "archaic" periods of all the great cultures. In such early periods the religious foundation of culture is all-pervasive, but it tends to be mythological and primitive. The rational protest against such forms of theonomy is justified. A new theonomy must be sought after the development of secular rationality and after the realization of independence by the various segments of culture.

In a mature theonomy the unconditional depth shines through all finite creations. At the same time, there is no conflict between religion and reason, between depth and rational structure. In connection with the previous discussion one may say that in a mature theonomy Spiritual Community has become normative for an entire culture. In Tillich's view this will be achieved only fragmentarily on the plane of human history.

In Tillich's view the protest of reason against an archaic theonomy produces a second type of culture, one characterized by "autonomy." This culture seeks to found itself upon the dictates of reason alone, "without any reference to something ultimate and unconditional."[5] In an autonomous culture many

---

[5]*Ibid.*, p. 57.

avenues of creativity are opened for man. He is "on his own," free to develop his potentialities in all directions. He sets his own standards, conceives and works toward his own goals. Freedom and self-discipline are the positive marks of this culture. The great sacred myths which had given unity to the culture are replaced by rationalized forms of social integration and cooperation. In an autonomous culture each area of human interest and activity tends to view itself as self-sufficient and self-governing. Philosophy and science reject theonomous presuppositions; art asserts its independence of religion; morality depends upon utilitarian and pragmatic calculations. This culture is not necessarily irreligious, but its religion tends to be individualistic and rationalistic. Religion is viewed as one segment of the culture, not as the unifying element in the entire culture.

The impulse toward autonomy is one of the major driving forces in human history and can never properly be repressed. However, the full realization of this type of culture has inevitable tragic results. According to Tillich, the more autonomy develops, the more spiritually empty the culture becomes. Having cut itself away from the concern for ultimates, it tends more and more to lose the sense of meaning and purpose. All values come to be viewed as finite and relative; nothing is of unconditional significance. In more advanced stages skepticism and cynicism become prevalent moods. Although an era of autonomy may be one of unprecedented technological advance, it is at the same time an era in which the "spiritual substance" of an earlier theonomy is continually wasted. Tillich considers the eighteenth-century Age of Enlightenment to have been a period of creative autonomy and the late nineteenth century a time when the dominant autonomy began to be revealed as sterile and empty.

The third type of culture described by Tillich appears as a reaction against autonomous trends. A culture (or segments thereof) which is experiencing the dissolution of its theonomy, but which shrinks from the dangers of autonomy, finds itself drawn to what Tillich calls "heteronomy." This term suggests an alien law imposed upon man from the outside in opposition to the dictates of his own reason. A culture is heteronomous when an authoritarian church, political party, or government seeks to suppress autonomous impulses and to impose an artificial uniformity of thought in the name of some ultimate. These social authorities may represent the insights of a past theonomy. Their leaders may understandably fear the loss of spiritual substance which accompanies autonomy. However, the heteronomous reaction can never be a satisfactory solution to the problem; it violates truth and justice and destroys human freedom. It can, and frequently does, lead to tyranny and fanaticism. In the authoritarian church of the late Middle Ages all of these features were present.

The conflict between autonomy and heteronomy gives rise to the "quest for a new theonomy."[6] In the absence of theonomy an increasingly sterile autonomy will provoke the appearance of new heteronomies representing false ultimates (such as nation or race). The rise of Naziism is interpreted by Tillich as a heteronomous reaction to the spiritually empty autonomous culture of nineteenth-century Europe. This destructive cycle of heteronomy and autonomy is unavoidable unless a new form of theonomy can be discovered. However, in Tillich's conception there is an element of grace in the coming of theonomy; it can be awaited with hope, but it cannot be forced.

The concept of theonomy is one of Tillich's central ideas. This can be seen in his summary of its characteristics: "Theonomy unites the absolute and the relative element in the interpretation of history, the demand that everything relative become the vehicle of the absolute and the insight that nothing relative can ever become absolute itself."[7] First, Tillich's assertion that anything may become "the vehicle of the absolute" is the basis for his analysis of symbols. Since all beings are rooted in being-itself, any being may become the medium for revealing the power of being. The history of religions shows that a wide variety of beings (including persons, natural beings, forces of nature, and human artifacts) have been considered revelatory. Tillich takes all of these claims seriously but notes at the same time a demonic possibility. That which is a vehicle for the ultimate may come

---

[6]Tillich, *Systematic Theology*, III, p. 252.
[7]Tillich, *The Protestant Era*, p. 47. Used by permission.

to be considered ultimate itself. In this fashion, that which was potentially revelatory may become in fact a source of idolatry.

Idolatry is prevented by the second characteristic of theonomy, "the insight that nothing relative can ever become absolute itself." This rule is our now familiar "Protestant principle." In Tillich's view the essential principle developed by Protestantism is the protest against any absolutizing of that which is relative. The original Protestant protest was against the absolutizing of the authority of the church, but Tillich believes that the principle has a broader application. The Protestant churches sought to reinstate another absolute in the form of the infallible Bible; whenever this happens, the Protestant principle must again be applied. The establishment of an unquestionable human authority is always heteronomous in Tillich's view. Religious authority derives from the actual mediation of the divine Presence. A true medium of religious insight points beyond itself; when it points to itself (or becomes itself the focus of religious devotion), it becomes an idol.

It is clear from this discussion that in Tillich's approach Jesus as the Christ was individually "theonomous." He was completely open and transparent to the eternal, but he did not claim absoluteness for himself in his finitude. Indeed, his willingness to sacrifice that which was finite in himself made it possible for his life to be fully revelatory. The crucifixion completes and thus becomes a symbol for this characteristic of Jesus' life.

One other feature of the concept of theonomy must be noted. There is an obvious similarity between Tillich's description of the emergence of a culture from its theonomous background and the emergence of man from his "original" unity with the divine life. Archaic theonomy parallels the condition of finite potentiality within the divine life. The destructive alteration between autonomy and heteronomy parallels the situation of man in estrangement alternating between lonely isolation and submergence in the social collective. The quest for a new theonomy is the social form of the quest for salvation. In both cases actual salvation is a "gift of God," not a human achievement. Thus there is a significant similarity between the development of the individual and the historical development of an individual culture. It is interesting to note, however, that both archaic and mature theonomy appear (at least fragmentarily) in actual history. Conversely, when Tillich discusses the stage of individual human potentiality, he emphasizes that this is a stage "prior to" actual existence—a kind of symbolic time which is no time. On the basis of this comparison we may suggest viewing the earlier stages of actual individual development as periods of at least relative potentiality. The distinction between relative potentiality (infancy) and relative actuality (maturity) can help us at least to conceive pure potentiality. There is, of course, no pure potentiality (or pure salvation) in existence as there is no pure theonomy in history. (The one exception is the Christ as seen by daring faith. It is here that the "beginning" and the "end" of man are most clearly seen.) Both salvation and theonomy can, however, be fragmentarily realized in moments of grace.

We must now comment upon the relation between Spiritual Community, the cultural types, and the institutional churches. We have remarked upon Tillich's understanding of life in general as inescapably ambiguous (combining positive and negative processes). This ambiguity reaches its height in human religion. It is to be expected, then, that Tillich's analysis of religion will be highly complex. Tillich views religion, on the one hand, as one of the central functions of the human spirit. Religion as the quest for the ultimate or for transcendence of the finite is found in all human life. Understood in this way, it is both an aspect of all human activities and itself a special activity. But religion as a function of man, as man's natural self-transcendence, remains a question and a quest. It cannot reach that for which it strives: union with the divine or unambiguous life.

However, religion is not simply a human quest; it also comes into being as the human response to divine revelation. Wherever revelation occurs, it forms Spiritual Community. This unambiguous response to revelation cannot be identified exclusively with any social institution, as we have seen. It may occur outside the churches as well as within the churches. But Spiritual Community outside the churches is latent; it lacks the ultimate criterion of revelation derived from the Christ-event, a criterion which gives to the actual churches a principle of self-criticism. Thus, Tillich concludes that one central distinguishing mark of the Christian church is its power of self-criticism. He states this quite strongly:

Nevertheless, church history has one quality which no other history has: since it relates itself in all its periods and appearances to the central manifestation of the Kingdom of God in history, it has in itself the ultimate criterion against itself—the New Being in Jesus as the Christ. The presence of this criterion elevates the churches above any other religious group, not because they are "better" than others, but because they have a better criterion against themselves and, implicitly, also against other groups.[8]

The churches, then, like all other human institutions and activities, are an ambiguous mixture of good and evil. Only in their transcendence of themselves are they superior to other institutions. (It might be noted parenthetically that the Roman Catholic Church in our time is applying this principle to itself. It is not confined to Protestantism!)

The churches then "represent the Spiritual Community in a manifest religious self-expression."[9] However, this expression is ambiguous; it is at once the actualization and the distortion of Spiritual Community. Tillich suggests that Spiritual Community may be considered the "essence" of the churches. Like the process of all life, the existing churches both actualize and distort their essence. Essence can be only fragmentarily realized in actual existence.

One further observation needs to be made. In Tillich's view the very existence of religious institutions as a separate cultural function is a sign of man's fallenness. In the kingdom of God there will be no "Temple"; in the fulfillment of history all elements of culture will be aware of their sacred depth. The actual culture which comes nearest to this ideal is the theonomous culture. In this culture the churches represent something which is implicit in all areas of the culture. In an autonomous

---

[8]Tillich, *Systematic Theology*, III, p. 381. Used by permission.
[9]*Ibid.*, p. 153.

culture the churches seem to be unnecessary appendages. In a heteronomous situation the claims made for the churches are inevitably idolatrous and demonic. Thus, only in a theonomous culture can the church truly be itself. Church and culture alike must hope for a new theonomy.

In summary, religion is tragic insofar as it is a human quest; it is ambiguous insofar as it is a response to divine revelation. Revelation in all history creates latent Spiritual Community. The Christian churches, created in response to the central revelation (though also containing elements of human religion), represent Spiritual Community in manifest form, but they distort it as well. The distinctive characteristic of the churches is their possession of a self-correcting norm. Only in a theonomous culture can the church realize its essence and become itself. This analysis may seem unduly complicated to account for the familiar church on the corner; yet Tillich is grappling with crucial issues. How can the church claim to represent the truth in the face of its obvious and glaring weaknesses? To what extent can the church claim uniqueness in a time of increasing awareness of other religions? What should be the Christian's attitude toward secular movements which at points seem to speak for God more effectively than the churches? These and other questions which modern man must ask can be answered in part in terms of Tillich's categories.

CHAPTER IX

The "End" of History and Eschatology

CHRISTIAN DOCTRINE must concern itself, finally, with questions about the "end." This discussion is usually classified as "eschatology," or the doctrine of last things. Tillich notes a dual meaning in the word "end": It signifies both "finish" and "aim." Eschatology is concerned both with the conclusion of things and with the inner aim of all things. Tillich's emphasis falls upon the latter concern. Furthermore, questions concerning the end are posed both in an individual and in a collective sense. Questions are asked both about the destiny of individuals and about the final meaning and aim of human history. Let us consider the latter problem first.

We cannot deal adequately here with Tillich's treatment of the ambiguities of history or with the way in which he presents Christian doctrine as an answer to these ambiguities.[1] It is possible to say in summary that he analyzes history in terms of the dynamics which he finds in life in all dimensions. History, like all life, is self-transcendent; this is the source of its greatness and its ambiguity.

In the historical dimension, life moves out of itself toward the future. History takes place in both time and space, but time is the dominant factor. The movement of history is irreversibly forward toward the new. History drives beyond the achievements of all individuals and groups. It moves beyond all relative creations of culture and forces man to ask the question of a final and non-relative fulfillment of time. Man's conscious par-

---

[1] Cf. Tillich, *Systematic Theology*, III, Part V, "History and the Kingdom of God."

ticipation in history leads him to the question of the goal of history.

Tillich sees three characteristic types of historical ambiguity.[2] First, life drives toward total unification or integration. This unifying tendency is manifested in the growth of nations and empires. This movement is tragic, however, in its tendency toward the destruction or curtailment of individual freedom and creativity. The question of an unambiguous unification which preserves individuality is a perennial problem in actual history. Second, life pushes forward toward the creation of the new. But tragically the realization of the new involves the destruction of the old. Revolution tends inevitably to threaten the genuine values of the old order. The question of an unambiguous creativity must be raised.

The third ambiguity is in the quest of life for an ultimate within time. History has seen repeated conflicts between those loyal to an absolute value and those opposed to it. Man must ask the question of an unambiguous ultimate. According to Tillich the Christian symbol of "the kingdom of God" can be presented effectively as an answer to these ambiguities of history. The kingdom of God, in Tillich's interpretation of the New Testament concept, points in two directions: It represents the ultimate fulfillment of history which at the same time appears fragmentarily within history. In his theological vocabulary it is immanent in Spiritual Presence and Spiritual Community, and it points to the transcendent reality of Eternal Life.

Tillich sees four characteristics of the symbol "the kingdom of God" which make it an effective representation of the culmination of history. First, it is political. It points both to the power of God (as "king") and to the "realm of the divine rule . . . a transformed heaven and earth, a new reality in a new period of history."[3] Here reappears the idea of the new creation. The present reality is not negated but is to be transformed and fulfilled. Second, this symbol is social and, hence, moral. It is an order in which peace and justice prevail. Third, it is personalistic. "In contrast to symbols in which the return to the ulti-

[2]Cf. *ibid.*, pp. 339-346.
[3]*Ibid.*, p. 358.

mate identity is the aim of existence, the Kingdom of God gives eternal meaning to the individual person."[4] We shall return to this theme in a moment. Finally, it is universal. It includes not only all men but nature as well.

Tillich believes this vision of the final aim of human history to be superior to all others. In the emerging encounter of the religions of the world with one another, the symbol of the kingdom of God will serve to protect these central affirmations of the Christian tradition. These values have political and social, as well as religious, relevance in our time.

For most Christians the question of the destiny of individuals is one of more crucial interest. We must now investigate Tillich's approach to the theme of eternal life as far as individuals are concerned.

Tillich's approach to the final destiny of man (and of all beings) is based upon his fundamental distinction between eternal life and everlasting life. Tillich urges repeatedly that participation in eternity is quite different from the continuation of existence through an endless time. He is unequivocal in his view that the latter concept, taken literally as a survival of finite life in a heaven or hell, is a superstition which must be rejected. The phrases "life after death" or "the life hereafter," insofar as they suggest a continuation of temporal life, are misleading and should be avoided.

Many readers, discovering these themes in Tillich's thought, conclude that he has no positive conception of man's final destiny. This conclusion, however, is incorrect. Tillich is simply convinced that the Christian hope is not properly expressed in terms of the endurance of the finite for an infinite time, whether this is expressed in terms of the "immortality of the soul" or the "resurrection of the body." Rather, man's destiny according to Christian faith must be conceived as a participation in God's eternal life. Tillich maintains that eternity is not everlasting time; it is the transcendence of time. The Christian hope, therefore, is that finite life may be elevated into eternal life. (It may

---

4*Ibid.*

be noted that Tillich's vocabulary in discussing this matter is closest to the Gospel of John.)

Approached in this way the traditional question concerning life after death may be reformulated. Tillich asks, "What aspects of existence can be elevated into the transcendent unity of the divine life?" He answers, first, that eternity is not the negation of finitude; when the finite is taken into the eternal, only the negative aspects of finitude are overcome and eliminated. The positive aspects of existence are "saved" and brought to fulfillment. What then are these positive aspects? Tillich's answer is in terms of his concept of life. The movement of finitude outside the divine life was seen as a movement from potentiality within the divine life toward actualization. However, negative as well as positive aspects of this movement were recognized. Destructive and self-contradictory trends appear in existence. Tillich understands the final or eschatological movement as "essentialization," or that movement which brings finite existence to fulfillment. This consummation involves the actualization of essence or potentiality enriched by the struggles and conflicts of existence in freedom. Only the destructive and self-negating tendencies of life are eliminated. In Tillich's view everything positive is gathered up into the divine life; nothing of value is lost.

What then is the destiny of self-conscious selves? Tillich's statement is that "the self-conscious self cannot be excluded from Eternal Life."[5] The realization of individual centers of consciousness is a good which must be taken up into the transcendent unity of the divine life. In Tillich's view individuality is not eliminated in the eternal. It is preserved in polar relationship with universal participation (or unification). In other words, the unity in the eternal is in the form of love, where individuality is the prerequisite for interpersonal union. On the other hand, the conscious self is not preserved in the same form as in earthly existence. Tillich denies that the participation of the self in eternal life can be conceived as an "endless continuation of a particular stream of consciousness in memory and anticipation."[6] There must be some transformation of the temporal self, but

[5]*Ibid.*, p. 413.
[6]*Ibid.*, p. 414.

further conceptualization of the form this actually takes is impossible.

Another feature of Tillich's approach should be noted. His concept of the transcendence of time should not be interpreted as the negation of temporality. In Tillich's conception, time, like the other aspects of finitude, is at once included in the divine life and transcended. In the title sermon of his collection entitled *The Eternal Now*, he draws an analogy which may be helpful.[7] Every human being has the experience of a stable "present," although time never pauses to give this present any actual extent. In a sense we are in time and yet transcend it in the experience of the present. Tillich suggests that this experience is possible only on the basis of participation in the eternal. Those, however, who are not aware of the presence of the eternal tend to lose their grasp upon the stable present and find themselves immersed in endless change and flux. The true experience of a serene present is a foretaste of that participation in "the eternal now" where temporality is at once accepted and transcended. This may be symbolized by saying that the finite remains present to God in his "eternal memory." However, God's memory, unlike that of man, is a "living retention of the remembered thing."[8]

Tillich's view of the theme of "last judgment" requires a brief comment. In summary, he holds that in the final consummation the negative features of existence will be purged, both individually and universally, and the positive aspects gathered into the unity of eternal life. This means that he rejects the idea of the absolute condemnation of some individual human beings and the absolute salvation of others. The traditional imagery of separating the "sheep and the goats" is applied by Tillich to the absolute separation of good and evil. No human being, however, can be considered absolutely good or absolutely evil. In Tillich's view his approach does not negate the seriousness of the "last judgment." One rightly feels grief and shame in contemplating the fact that much of his being is dross, with no eternal significance. At the same time, one who experiences the

---

[7]Cf. Tillich, *The Eternal Now*, pp. 122-132.
[8]Tillich, *Systematic Theology*, III, p. 399.

despair of condemnation must be shown that he, too, can share in the joy of fulfillment. Tillich's point is that no absolute judgments can be made concerning finite beings or events. This is the truth which he sees in theological "universalism," the doctrine that all beings will finally be saved.

Tillich's discussion is a positive and constructive reconsideration of the Christian tradition concerning "last things." No doubt obscurities remain, as may be expected. Those who demand a more affirmative approach to the question of the endurance of the soul or the revival of the body must be reminded of the dangers of wishful thinking and sentimentality. In all such discussions symbolic material is involved. But surely Tillich is correct in maintaining that some symbols are more appropriate than others—appropriate either in expressing the essential content of religious intuition or in preserving intellectual integrity. Tillich makes a convincing case for a new vocabulary in this area.

CHAPTER X

The Ongoing Debate:

TILLICH CRITICIZED

A COMPREHENSIVE SYSTEM of thought like Tillich's would be expected to provoke widespread critical comment. A system *invites* criticism in a way that occasional essays do not. The application of a single framework of interpretation to diverse areas of experience and thought leaves the system vulnerable to criticism by specialists in each of these areas. Indeed, this provoking of critical thinking is one of the major functions of a systematic construction.

Many scholars, both young and old, have sharpened their critical tools by giving careful scrutiny to various aspects of Tillich's thought. These appraisals, coming as they do from widely diverse perspectives, vary greatly in their evaluation of Tillich's achievement. Also, most of them thus far have been piecemeal studies. A balanced judgment concerning Tillich's enduring place in the history of philosophy and of Christian thought probably remains some years in the future.

In this study it is not possible even to identify all of the problem areas in Tillich's thought. Rather, the author has selected several areas where, in his judgment, the criticism of Tillich is most interesting and the reservations expressed about his position most valid. This is admittedly a subjective judgment; other writers, no doubt, would select other areas for consideration.

We shall begin with a few comments concerning a philosophical appraisal. It is significant that Tillich's theology has aroused the interest of some philosophers who otherwise give little attention to theology. Although the judgments made by these philosophers are frequently negative, these discussions can nevertheless provide a strong stimulus to the philosophy of religion.

One of the central interests of contemporary philosophy is the analysis of language—the examination of the various ways in which words are used. According to the language analysts, the main function of philosophy is the achievement of clarity as to what our words actually mean in the different realms of discourse. This type of analysis has been made of the language of metaphysics and of theology (as well as discussion of moral values and of aesthetics, for example). Tillich's complex interweaving of metaphysical and theological language has therefore proved fascinating to these analysts.

We cannot deal here with the general argument of some philosophers of language that there are no distinctive meanings in the realms of metaphysical and theological discourse—that statements in these fields are strictly meaningless insofar as they are not reducible to statements of empirical fact. This challenge to theology (as well as metaphysics) deserves careful consideration. There is growing evidence that a constructive dialogue is possible between the "second generation" language analysts (whose conclusions are not quite so sweeping) and those theologians who are willing to acknowledge the need for greater clarity as to what their words mean.[1] One more specific criticism of Tillich's language arising from this school of thought may properly concern us here.

Tillich has been accused of a kind of obscurity which Professor Paul Edwards identifies as a "bombastic redescription of familiar facts."[2] This charge deserves attention even if one does not assume that theological statements are meaningful only when they can be reduced to empirical fact. The question naturally occurs to the average reader: Can Tillich's insights be stated more simply, or is his complex, technical vocabulary essential to the content of his work?

---

[1] Cf. the study of this problem by William Hordern: *Speaking of God: The Nature and Purpose of Theological Language* (New York: The Macmillan Company, 1964).

[2] Paul Edwards, "Professor Tillich's Confusions," *Mind*, LXXIV, No. 294 (April, 1965), p. 207.

Edwards asserts, for example, that Tillich's elaborate discussion of the "threat of nonbeing" can be reduced to discussion about death as an empirical fact. He argues that Tillich's use of the term "nonbeing" is deceptive; it appears to be a name for something when actually it only points to certain "negativities" in experience. When one states, "No one is at the door," he does not mean that there is a shadowy something called "no one" at the door. To be threatened by "nothing" is not to have an actual antagonist who can be described.[3]

It may be observed first that this sort of analysis can be very helpful. Tillich's ontological terminology is not particularly appealing to the American religious public. If his language could be simplified, his thought could be made available to a much wider audience. There are pitfalls, however, in such simplification. To return to Edwards' illustration, it is doubtful that Tillich's full meaning is preserved when "nonbeing" is reduced to "death." Tillich observes that the meaning of the word "death" is always colored by its opposite, "life." In ordinary usage only living beings are subject to death. Tillich intends a wider application of the concepts of life and death. By analogy all beings are subject to the kind of dissolution which in the realm of living beings is referred to as death. (There are also forms of dissolution in the human realm which do not involve physical death, e.g., psychic disintegration or moral degradation. Tillich would include these in his wider application.) Furthermore, it has been said of living things that they die a little in each moment of life. This too, Tillich thinks, is true by extension of all finite beings. Indeed, he suggests, this is the meaning of finitude. One way of expressing this idea is to say that all finite beings are "mixed with nonbeing" or are "threatened by nonbeing." This life is then contrasted with the idea of eternal life—a life which continually overcomes the threat of nonbeing.

It is true that this whole development of thought is rooted in the human experience of facing death. However, Tillich has used this experience as the basis for a concept which applies to all beings. It is true that when one attempts to explain Tillich's

---

[3]Cf., *ibid.*, pp. 206-214.

meaning, he finds himself referring to the facing of death as a concrete application of the idea of nonbeing. But Tillich has employed the ontological vocabulary to indicate the universality of the concept. No doubt some confusion results from the complex elaboration of the idea of nonbeing. At times it seems to take on the properties of a metaphysical substance. This confusion suggests the possibility that another vocabulary, both in this and other such cases, may serve the ends of greater clarity. However, it is not at all apparent that a word which has a specific empirical reference is superior to a more abstract term with a wider application. In any case, it will certainly be appropriate for American theologians to attempt to express Tillich's insights in an alternative vocabulary. In this attempt the concepts of linguistic analysis may prove very helpful.

Another aspect of Tillich's approach to theological language which has aroused great interest is his view that all terms describing God must be "symbolic" (with one possible exception to be mentioned). This is an issue of great importance in the theological world, and it is one to which considerable attention has been given in recent theology. Furthermore, Tillich's position has proved confusing to the general religious public. To admit that one is talking in symbols seems to be a kind of double-talk: What one is saying is both true and not true. Because of the importance of the issue and the possibility of confusion, we should like to examine Tillich's position here in some detail. It will be necessary to explain some features of Tillich's analysis before we can seek to evaluate it. This can perhaps best be done by separating the philosophical and the religious aspects of Tillich's treatment of symbols.

Tillich's approach to God may be described on the philosophical side as a combination of Kantianism and mysticism. Quite fundamental to his understanding of God is his assertion that the ultimate or unconditional lies "beyond the subject-object relationship." Discussion of the subject-object relationship is prominent in Kant and in the post-Kantian philosophies. The phrase refers to the view that ordinary perception and thought have two components: the knowing mind (the subject) and the content which is presented to the mind by the senses (the objects). Every finite thing appears to us in the subject-object relationship. In Tillich's view (and here he is in agreement with Kant as well as with ancient and modern mysticism), God as the unconditional cannot appear within the subject-object relationship. This means to Tillich that God cannot appear to man as either subject or object, as either self or thing in any literal sense. (Here, of course, many theologians disagree. They maintain that God is not known as an object, but he is known as subject, as person.)

Since man's languages are oriented toward the subject-object world, they are inadequate to describe this "beyond." Seeking nevertheless to identify that to which our inadequate terms apply, Tillich draws upon the Western ontological tradition. The unconditional which is neither subject nor object is "being-itself," the ultimate reality sought by many philosophers. Tillich thus maintains that the statement "God is being-itself" is one of the basic assertions of theology.[4] Since being-itself is the "ground" or source of both selves and the objects of which selves are aware, it cannot be properly conceptualized as either subject or object. Since these exhaust the finite alternatives, no description of being-itself can be literally true. Tillich agrees with mysticism in its assertion that being-itself is known not through conceptualization but only through "participation"— through the experience of unity or oneness with the Divine. The concepts which we use to describe being-itself are symbolic; they are not literally true, but they are valid if they provide a medium for the experience of unity with the ground of being.

Tillich has engaged in a debate with himself and others as to whether the statement "God is being-itself" is itself non-symbolic. He first affirmed this to be the case and then later suggested rather ambiguously that the statement is the point where the "symbolic and the non-symbolic coincide."[5] One suggestion which Tillich makes concerning theology may help to

---

[4]Tillich, *Systematic Theology,* I, pp. 238-239.
[5]Tillich, *Systematic Theology,* II, p. 10.

illuminate his position. Theologians "must begin with the most abstract and completely unsymbolic statement which is possible, namely, that God is being-itself or the absolute."[6] When his point is expressed in this fashion, one appears to be confronted with a definition of the word God. The definition may be rendered in the famous phrase of St. Anselm: God is "that than which nothing greater can be conceived." It would seem quite proper and appropriate to define God in this way; but one must then recall that Anselm's effort to prove that such a being must exist has been judged a failure. We remain in the realm of concept.

The statement "God is being-itself" may be alternatively interpreted in this way: The reality which Christians profess to have encountered in religious experience is being-itself or the absolute—"that than which nothing greater can be conceived." One might question whether this truth is necessarily contained in the religious experience. Is that which is experienced as ultimate for me necessarily ultimate in being? It would appear that an additional assertion is present here: Only that which is truly ultimate in being can be the *proper* object of ultimate loyalty or concern for me. This implicit assertion leads Tillich to the position that all concrete ultimates (moral laws, divine commands, final meanings, etc.) are symbols for being-itself or the ultimate reality. It is doubtful that this apprehension is contained in all religious experience. Rather, it is a specific article of faith.

Let us repeat: Something is experienced as ultimate for me (and for my group); I (or we) call this reality "God." But I know (intuitively? as a philosophical *a priori?*) that God must be the ultimate reality, the source of all being. Nothing less than this could truly be God. This knowledge is, once again, Tillich's Protestant principle: Only God can be God; only the ultimate reality can rightly be worshiped. We suggested earlier that the Protestant principle is derived, according to Tillich, from the impact of the self-sacrificing life of Christ upon the church. Christianity knows what other religions presumably do not know:

---

[6]Tillich, *Systematic Theology*, I, p. 239.

that the finite can reveal the Divine only by sacrificing itself, only by removing the finite in itself.

Tillich's statement "God is being-itself," then, is a definition of God. But it is a definition which is rooted in Christian experience—not only the experience of being grasped by an ultimate concern (this is characteristic of all religions), but the experience of being grasped by an ultimate concern whose medium negates itself in its finitude so that nothing finite can be worshiped. Hence comes the Christian assertion: God can be no finite being; he can be nothing less than the ultimate reality. It is apparently the *concept* of ultimate reality which Tillich holds to be nonsymbolic. The concept seems to involve the notion of standing "beyond the subject-object relationship." But to speak of a *being* as ultimate, one must in some sense experience ultimacy. It would appear that the only way of doing this is in the Christian experience of finding ultimacy in that which explicitly renounces its own claim to ultimacy. In this experience the Christian is united with the ultimate and knows that the ultimate transcends the finite (the subject-object world). If this analysis is correct, the statement "God is being-itself" is a formal definition of God drawn from Christian experience.

When we leave the realm of conceptualization and speak of participation in or experience of being-itself, we have turned from philosophy to religion. (Mysticism indeed provides a bridge between the two.) We must now comment upon Tillich's understanding of symbols insofar as this is expressed in religious terms. Tillich maintains that all knowledge of God or being-itself is the result of "revelation," or the experience of being "grasped by an ultimate concern." Revelation occurs when some concrete event, object, or interpersonal relationship becomes "transparent" to its own ground and thus reveals the unity of finitude with being-itself. This may occur, for example, in the apprehension of a moral imperative, in an aesthetic experience, or in a recognition of some ultimate meaning. In every case that by which one is grasped is apprehended as ultimate and unconditional. Tillich argues that all constructive philosophies (as distinguished from purely analytical philosophy) are based upon some concrete revelation no less than religion. All revelation is fragmentary and incomplete (although this does not prevent us from affirming in daring faith that a certain revelation is normative).

The concrete medium of revelatory experience becomes in Tillich's terms a symbol for the ultimate reality. In man's history, symbols for the Divine have been drawn from the whole range of human experience. They may be sacred objects, personified forces of nature, social institutions which are considered holy, sacred books, or sets of relatively abstract ideas. All represent the ultimate in concrete form; all are symbols.

Does this mean that all symbols for the ultimate are equally valid? Is Tillich placing all religions and all fanatical obsessions on the same level? In one sense the answer is yes. All faiths, however narrow or perverted, are based upon the experience of being grasped by an ultimate concern. As Tillich suggests: "In this qualified sense God is the fundamental and universal content of faith."[7] The experience of having an ultimate value is the same in all faiths, however different and even antithetical the values may be. The symbol which occasions or produces an ultimate concern is effective in representing the ultimate and is in that sense valid. Tillich seems to say that if any aspect of reality is experienced as possessing ultimacy, this experience is self-authenticating and not subject to question.

Tillich proposes to evaluate symbols in a way quite different from a judgment concerning their truth or falsity. He asks whether a symbol becomes "demonic" in its reception by man and in its function in human life. Tillich has developed the idea of the demonic in several different forms, but it is best explained in terms of the biblical concept of "idolatry." An idol is a finite reality (whether a part of nature or a human creation) which is invested with the power or holiness of God. The central religious conflict of the Old Testament, for example, is that between the worship of Yahweh, the Lord of Israel, and the worship of the Canaanite Baal, the latter interpreted by the prophets as idolatry —the worship of a finite reality in the place of the true God.

In Tillich's interpretation a symbol for God (and this may be any portion of finite reality) becomes demonic (an idol) when

[7]Tillich, *The Dynamics of Faith* (New York: Harper and Brothers, 1957), p. 46.

the claim is made that this finite being is itself divine. To avoid idolatry, symbols for God must point beyond themselves to the ground of being and meaning. This means that they must be recognized as symbols, as media of revelation which are not themselves the reality but which point to it. This is the basis for Tillich's surprising statement: "Faith, if it takes its symbols literally, becomes idolatrous!"[8]

One may ask what is meant by recognizing a representation of God as symbolic. Tillich might reply in terms of his concept of theonomy. There is an early stage in the development of culture when the distinction between literal and symbolic is not made. This stage would be the period of archaic theonomy mentioned earlier, where every finite reality seems transparent to a holy depth. Here there are no special symbols for the Divine, for in a sense everything is "symbolic"—one is immediately aware of the mystery of being in every encounter with reality. It is proper to say that for Tillich this condition of theonomy is also the goal of human existence. This goal can be achieved only after the early period has been broken by development of the critical intellect. Reason demythologizes and purges the finite gods; those that resist criticism do so only through some authoritarian structures (heteronomy). But in Tillich's view symbols cannot be eliminated. They must be "broken," recognized for what they are; then their true power can be manifest while their demonic characteristics are overcome.

Tillich therefore recommends a "dialectical" approach to symbols—an approach which at the same time affirms and negates their validity.[9] It is not always clear what this approach entails. It may mean that the characteristic of God asserted by the symbol must be affirmed along with its polar opposite. For example, one may affirm that God is an individual (as in the assertion that he is personal) if one at the same time affirms that he participates universally in all things. Since God is beyond the polarity of individuality and participation, it is possible to apply each characteristic to God in conjunction with the other.

---

[8]*Ibid.*, p. 52.
[9]Tillich, *Systematic Theology*, I, p. 239.

The dialectical approach, however, may also mean the affirmation of the symbol along with the negation of all that is finite in the symbol. This is the more important, but also the more difficult, meaning of dialectics. The negation of the purely finite is possible for man to conceive, according to Tillich, because man knows infinity although he is bound to finitude. We have dealt with this aspect of man in our discussion of self-transcendence. A symbol drawn from the human realm may be affirmed of God in its self-transcending meaning while being denied of God in its finite meaning. For example, when the word "life" is applied to God, this cannot mean that God grows and decays like finite life. But man by virtue of his humanity glimpses and indeed fragmentarily shares in eternal life beyond finitude. It is this life, which man possesses only by sharing in God's life, which must be affirmed of God. In Tillich's expression the symbol gains its validity from participation in that which it symbolizes. The symbol of life is drawn from finitude, but from a finitude which transcends itself and shares in that which it seeks to symbolize. According to Tillich we could not know God at all if we were not partially at one with him. Finite entities could not be used to symbolize divinity if they did not share in divinity. A symbol points to that in finitude which is beyond finitude. If God is called "Father," this means not only that God is like man in this respect but also that fatherhood in essence is divine, that it has an eternal meaning.[10]

An effective symbol for God, then, according to Tillich, must contain the negation of its own finitude. It is for this reason that the cross of Christ is the most powerful symbol for the presence of God. Jesus consciously sacrificed all that was finite in himself in order that the divinity in him might be manifested. The crucifixion of Jesus was the culmination of a life of self-sacrifice which enabled him to be the revealer. In reality it is the life of Jesus which is the symbol, in Tillich's sense. This does not mean that his life was unreal or nonhistorical. It means that by giving up all claims for the ultimacy of his finitude Jesus effectively represented and manifested the Divine within

---

[10]Cf. *ibid.*, p. 240.

the conditions of finite existence. Whenever absolute claims are made concerning his finitude, however, the figure of Jesus becomes an idol.

Tillich's analysis of symbols is an impressive treatment of a number of complex problems. No doubt it will be a major point of departure for discussions of religious symbolism for many years to come. Nevertheless, his approach leaves even the sympathetic reader with certain misgivings.

No doubt one basic reason for this dissatisfaction is the typical American preference for facts over "unfounded speculations." Our culture is prejudiced in favor of positivistic philosophies. This tendency is reconciled in the minds of many with literalistic religion. God is either a real being or he isn't; if he is, there must be positive and conclusive evidence to this effect. It is widely believed that this evidence was available to the biblical authors (in the form of visions, miracles, and the like) even if this evidence is not available to us in the same form. When a person of a literalistic persuasion is told that the biblical narratives concerning God are symbolic, it is tantamount to telling him that they are not true in any sense.

One must be entirely honest in dealing with such reactions. It must be recognized that in making the transition from a literal to a symbolic interpretation of statements about God, an entire understanding of God is being destroyed and another put in its place. It may be argued in a post-Freudian age that the former understanding is infantile or immature (a nonreligious type of argument, to be sure), but it is a view which has the advantage of clarity and simplicity. The man with the symbolic understanding of God seems to be cut adrift on a sea of uncertainty. If we encounter only mystery when we seek God, would it not be better to confine our attention to the finite world, which we can know in a reliable fashion? There are rebuttals for these arguments, but they have a powerful effect upon many Americans.

This hostility toward symbolism has been bolstered in recent years by a more reflective form of opposition. World War II and its aftermath have revealed again to mankind the appalling consequences of devotion to false absolutes. Symbols played an important role in the twentieth-century ideological movements such as Naziism. Some voices are now telling us that all symbols, as well as all ideologies (interpretations of human existence in terms of symbols), are dangerous. This thoroughgoing rejection of symbolism is nicely summed up in a statement by the German novelist, Gunter Grass, recently quoted in *Life* magazine:

Only ideologists need symbols to manifest themselves. Nazis with their swastikas, Communists with their hammers and sickles, the Roman Catholics with their arsenals full of images, the capitalists with their trademarks. I am even afraid of turning anti-ideology into an ideology. I just know what I want and don't want—the danger is when these things become a system.[11]

This is a strongly worded indictment of all symbols, but expressed somewhat more cautiously it would ring a responsive chord with many Americans. Symbols arouse the emotions and cloud our perception of the facts; it is, after all, more intelligent to seek short-range, practical goals without ideology and without self-deception.

Tillich's reply to this kind of argument might well take its point of departure from the same historical facts cited by those like Gunter Grass who oppose the use of symbols. Tillich asserts that twentieth-century man has rediscovered the power of symbols, though unfortunately their demonic power has been most forcefully illustrated. In Tillich's view the strength of a symbol is derived from its religious dimension, the power of the ultimate concern which it creates in those who receive it. A religious commitment can be criticized only from the standpoint of another religion; a symbol can be destroyed only in the power of another symbol. The twentieth century has witnessed the clash of rival ultimates and their symbols. The wars of our time in important respects have been religious wars, though in secular garb. In Tillich's opinion the effort to produce a culture devoid of symbols will fail; it will only create a vacuum into which the demonic absolutes will be drawn. To Tillich, Martin Luther was right: For man it is "either God or an idol."

---

[11]"Green Years for Grass," *Life* magazine (June 4). © 1965 Time Inc. Used by permission.

This dispute concerning man's need for symbols is an important debate and leads directly to the question: Is man incurably religious even when he consciously rejects overt religion? We shall want to consider the theological controversy on this matter, but let us first continue our evaluation of Tillich's approach to symbols. Even those who recognize the need for the use of symbolism in religion and who accept Tillich's argument that man cannot live without symbols for his ultimate concern may feel, nevertheless, that Tillich fails to provide adequate criteria for distinguishing one symbol from another. Can it be said that the main difference between the Nazi ideology of national and racial absolutism and the Christian worship of a just and loving personal Being is that the former claims ultimacy for itself while the latter "points beyond itself" to the true ultimate reality? It would appear, on the contrary, that too much weight is placed upon this one distinction. No doubt Tillich's analysis of idolatry is illuminating; no doubt the church must be warned against absolutizing its own symbols. But is not one symbol, relatively speaking, *truer* to the ultimate reality than another? Everyone will admit that none of our concepts is completely adequate to express the nature of the divine Being, but most would agree that some concepts are more adequate than others. On the basis of his approach to symbols, however, Tillich cannot really say this.

It would appear, furthermore, that Tillich does not actually confine himself to the understanding of symbols presented above. After having maintained that all language about God is symbolic and not to be judged in terms of its literal truth or falsity, Tillich proceeds to a very subtle and intricate metaphysical analysis of the divine nature. It is always difficult for the reader to remember that this analysis is to be considered symbolic, not literally true. Anyone can understand if it is said that fatherhood is attributed symbolically to God. But if God's fatherhood is examined in infinite detail, one begins to assume that we know more than we are letting on. If we know in detail the ways in which God's fatherhood differs from man's, we need not confine ourselves to the use of symbols.

Presumably, Tillich claims that his understanding of God (his analysis of the divine life, for instance) is truer than alternative views. If asked for the grounds upon which this claim is founded, would Tillich assert its superiority to lie in the fact that he does not claim his conceptions to be literally true? Surely, on the contrary, his conceptions are thought to be an approximation of the truth on the basis of certain rational or intuitive grounds. (No doubt Tillich's criterion of coherence is relevant here.)

It may be argued that Tillich's fundamental problem arises as a consequence of equating the philosophical object and the religious object—God as an object of knowledge and God as an object of worship. In terms of philosophy, God is beyond the subject-object relationship, and therefore no concepts drawn from the finite realm can adequately describe him. However, this does not prevent the effort to gain more adequate concepts (for example, through Tillich's dialectical approach). In terms of religion, it may be considered dangerous to identify God too closely with any aspect of finite experience. Any tendency to define and hence to delimit God must be criticized. Man's ultimate concern must be directed only toward that which is truly ultimate. The impulses of philosophy and religion, then, are partly opposed. Both seek ultimate reality. However, philosophy can accept the path of approximation, but religion must emphasize the discontinuity between the ultimate reality and every finite reality. Although religion finds God *in* the finite, it must not identify God *with* the finite. Philosophy, seeking more accurate conceptualization, ventures to identify God approximately with some features of finite reality. It does not accept an absolute discontinuity between the conditioned and the unconditional. Tillich's conceptualization of the divine life should be classified as philosophical approximation. As we have seen, it is a further step to affirm that the reality thus approximated is identical with the unconditional God of faith. In the statement, "God is being-itself," this identity is affirmed. Tillich has sought to formulate a concept of symbol which will fulfill the requirements of both areas. However, there are important differences between a symbol used in an effort to conceptualize the Divine and a symbol which functions as a mediator of the divine Presence. The continuing tension between these two functions of symbols in Tillich's system prevents his resolution of these problems from being entirely successful.

On the basis of our analysis of Tillich's understanding of symbols and in conjunction with our discussions of "ultimate concern," we can evaluate Tillich's approach to the historical records concerning Jesus. Christians for a century and a half have found it necessary to take an interest in the results of historical research dealing with the gospel records. Students of the New Testament, on the basis of generally accepted evidence, have agreed that the earliest Gospel was written a full generation after the death of Jesus. This fact inevitably suggests a question: To what extent are the Gospels accurate historical accounts of the life of Jesus? No one supposes that the Christian faith would be conclusively proved by a demonstration that the records are accurate, but many would admit that the faith could be seriously weakened by a demonstration that they are grossly inaccurate.

We have noted that Tillich in his youth took a great interest in the efforts of scholars to reconstruct the life of the "historical Jesus" behind the Gospels. He reached the conclusion that such efforts could never reach more than a certain degree of historical probability. The evidence is limited and inconclusive, even in comparison with other areas of historical research. Furthermore, Tillich decided, the matter of the historical Jesus is not the primary concern. Christianity has always based itself upon "the New Testament picture of Jesus as the Christ."[12] It is a certain fact, Tillich suggests, that a man (whose name was probably Jesus) was received as the Messiah, the bearer of the New Being, by the New Testament community. About this reception, he thinks, there can be no argument.

To describe this reception of Jesus in Tillich's categories, it could be said that the members of the early church community were grasped by an ultimate concern, that they were involved in an ecstatic reception of revelation. This, says Tillich, was im-

---

[12]Cf. Tillich, *Systematic Theology,* II, p. 123 and elsewhere.

mediately certain to them, and it is also immediately certain to those who participate in the historical continuation of this community. The latter groups throughout history are grasped by an ultimate concern which is mediated through the New Testament picture of Jesus as the Christ. This certainty does not include the claim that all of the historical details concerning Jesus recorded in the Gospels are accurate. Indeed, it seems probable that some of them are not.

It would seem that the only historical possibility which Tillich rules out is the possibility that the gospel records were cynically fraudulent imaginings, written with the intent to deceive. With this interpretation excluded, it is possible to say with confidence that the biblical writers and their fellows were grasped by an ultimate concern which was occasioned by their knowledge of Jesus. At this point we must remember that Tillich does not evaluate ultimate concerns by factual or scientific criteria. The ultimate concern is self-authenticating, except for the fact that the Protestant principle must be applied to it. This means that the only ultimate concern which does not become demonic is the one which is self-critical, which negates its own finitude. Thus in Tillich's view the ultimate concern occasioned by Jesus of Nazareth is self-authenticating and also contains its own principle of self-criticism. This ultimate concern can therefore be considered valid and normative without regard to the historical probabilities.

This is an interesting and helpful analysis, but it has certain limitations. Tillich has emphasized the passive side of faith: the experience of being grasped by an ultimate concern. When this aspect of faith is stressed, there can be no argument. I accept that by which I am grasped, whether this occurs through my encounter with a man (as with the first-century Christians) or through my encounter with the written records concerning this man and testimony about him (as with later Christians). But is not the passive aspect of faith in polar relation (to use a Tillichian phrase) with an active aspect, the quality of decision? Must I not make some judgment about that by which I am grasped and decide to give myself to it? If this is true, I must know as much as possible about that which grasped the New Testament community, and I must be concerned about the authenticity of the historical details.

This is an important issue in connection with Tillich's theology in its entirety. Tillich has urged that in man's relation to God, God is always active, and man is the recipient of God's action. At this point Tillich follows in the tradition of classical Reformation theology. But is this not a point at which theology must become dialectical? Must we not, with Paul, speak both of God working in us and of man working out his own salvation?[13] Tillich's principle of self-criticism may be relevant here. If the Christian takes the risk of faith in Jesus as the Christ, must he not also take the risk of a critical scrutiny of the figure of Jesus insofar as this is possible through historical research? One could argue that even in the matter of faith man's life combines destiny and freedom. Through his destiny man is grasped by an ultimate concern, but in his freedom man must affirm it. It would appear that in his treatment of the reception of Jesus by his followers (both contemporary and noncontemporary) Tillich does not give adequate place to man's freedom of critical inquiry into the very foundations of his faith.

Tillich, of course, acknowledges that historical research is important in establishing historical probabilities. This means that it has great importance in the realm of theology—in the formulation of faith. Historical study may, for example, lead to the rejection of some segments of the gospel record as unfactual. But Tillich holds that there can be no uncertainty about the unconditionality of an ultimate concern. Here all the stress is on the characteristic of faith as a "being grasped." Like Luther, he stresses the passive aspect of faith. Is it, however, unsound to find in faith an element of "making something ultimate for me" —an active aspect? For Tillich this is the activity of the Spirit in me. But one might argue that a dialectic of destiny and freedom might be more satisfactory here than an undialectical predestination.

---

[13]Cf. Philippians 2:12-13.

We noted that our discussion of symbolism brought us to the point of raising a more substantive anthropological and theological question. Is man ineradicably religious—is he *homo religiosus* by his very nature? Or are we observing in the twentieth century the emergence of a new breed: secular man, for whom religion in all forms is sheer anachronism and superstition? As we have seen, Tillich is clearly on the side of those who affirm, with Augustine, that all men have a thirst for the eternal and are restless until they find it. At this point Tillich stands in the mainstream of Christian thought on the subject. In recent years, however, a group of Christian theologians have arisen to challenge this view of man. The group received its initial impetus from the provocative but fragmentary writings of the German theologian and martyr, Dietrich Bonhoeffer (1906-1945).

Because of his opposition to Hitler, Bonhoeffer spent the last years of his life in a German concentration camp and was executed by the Nazis shortly before the war's end. During his years in prison he wrote a number of letters to relatives and friends. In these documents one can find sketches of a new understanding of modern man and his relation to religion.

In *Letters and Papers from Prison,* Bonhoeffer observes that in the modern period the hypothesis of God has become less necessary in many fields of inquiry. The relevance of the idea has been pushed back into the margins of life. God has become only "a stop-gap for the incompleteness of our knowledge."[14] In the twentieth century this process has neared its completion; in Bonhoeffer's now famous phrase, the world has "come of age." It can go about its daily affairs "without recourse to God as a working hypothesis."[15]

Religious thinkers, according to Bonhoeffer, have surrendered to secularism on all scientific problems but have asserted the continuing relevance of religion to the "ultimate" questions in the personal realm: such problems as guilt, suffering, and death. In relation to these areas, they say, man still needs religion because it provides the only solution to these problems. The real

---

[14]Bonhoeffer, *Letters and Papers from Prison* (New York: The Macmillan Company, 1962), p. 190.

[15]*Ibid.*, p. 195.

threat to religion in this age, then, comes from the men who seem to live happily and to "solve" these problems passably well without religion. In the face of this threat, says Bonhoeffer, religion has allied itself for apologetic purposes with that secular thought which seeks to uncover hidden human weaknesses. This type of material is available, for example, in the literature of existentialism and of psychoanalysis. Thus, Bonhoeffer writes:

> We have of course the secularized off-shoots of Christian theology, the existentialist philosophers and the psychotherapists, who demonstrate to secure, contented, happy mankind that it is really unhappy and desperate, and merely unwilling to realize that it is in severe straits it knows nothing at all about, from which only they can rescue it.[16]

Bonhoeffer categorically rejects the form of Christian apologetic theology which launches this kind of attack upon "the adulthood of the world" in order to prove that it is really weak and in need of salvation. This approach, he says, is ignoble, unaristocratic, and finally un-Christian. Christianity in a world come of age must recognize the fact that many men get along passably well without religion. The church must come to grips with mature secularism. Bonhoeffer therefore proposes that the understanding of the Christian gospel as a solution to individual problems be abandoned.

Bonhoeffer's constructive proposals are fragmentary and permit alternative interpretations. His central theme seems to be that the Christian man is not one who is preoccupied with his own problems; he is not the man who devotes himself to the quest for his own salvation. He is, rather, the man who is strong enough to act on behalf of others, to share in the suffering of the world. He is not the man who is seeking something, but the man who is giving something. The Christian is not offered the power of God to overcome his weakness; he is unexpectedly called upon to "participate in the sufferings of God at the hands of a godless world."[17] Christianity is misinterpreted when it is understood as a religion of salvation.

---

[16]*Ibid.*, p. 196. Used by permission of The Macmillan Company and Student Christian Movement Press, Ltd., London.

[17]*Ibid.*, p. 222.

This is a challenging critique of a number of themes in traditional theology, a critique made all the more powerful by the profoundly Christian life of the one who presents it. It is clear that Bonhoeffer includes Tillich among those who exploit human weaknesses in an unjustified fashion. It is, of course, true that Tillich uses existentialist and psychoanalytic material to establish man's estrangement and his need for salvation. Would we therefore judge Bonhoeffer's criticism to be justified? Does Tillich indulge in an ignoble attack upon the adulthood of the world?

In this writer's opinion Bonhoeffer's criticism may fairly be directed at Tillich's tendency to view despair as a prelude to faith. This theme is probably the product of Tillich's inclination to think dialectically and paradoxically. At points he suggests that the man who has reached the state of greatest estrangement is best prepared for reconciliation. All human securities must be stripped away before the truth can be found. For example, Tillich writes:

The fate of self-deception or—as Marx called it—of the production of ideologies is inescapable, except in selected groups which are predominantly composed of people in ultimate anxiety, despair and meaninglessness. On the boundary of all human possibilities the new possibility arises and gains power. If all ideological veils are torn down and self-deception is no longer possible, truth can appear and can be acted upon.[18]

This selection is an excerpt from an article on Marxism and perhaps should not be taken out of its context. But overtones of this same viewpoint appear in Tillich's general theological perspective. Tillich returns more than once to the theme that only the man who has lost all earthly securities is opened for the infinite.

It may be argued that Tillich's attraction to an Hegelian dialectical reversal (the Marxian crisis and revolution) leads him to an unrealistic psychology. Tillich himself knows that the condition of despair may, in fact, lead only to bitterness and

---

[18]Tillich, *The Protestant Era*, p. 255. Used by permission.

self-pity. Similarly, the presence of some earthly securities may enable one to think more clearly about the limitations of these securities. (Do healthy and supportive human relationships necessarily become idolatrous? Surely they do not.) There is a tendency in Tillich to view the condition of anguish or despair about the meaning of life as the most fertile ground for the reception of revelation. Insofar as this suggests a kind of indirect cultivation of despair, we may conclude that the point has been exaggerated. Dealing with actual anguish of spirit is one thing; cultivating it is another. To this extent Bonhoeffer's criticism would appear to be valid.

There is, however, another side to Tillich's thought. As we have seen, Tillich respects the autonomous man and the autonomous culture. He rejects the heteronomous effort to impose religion upon man from the outside in opposition to his true desires. He attacks autonomy only insofar as it tends to become sterile and empty. It is clear that he prefers a healthy autonomy to a dogmatic heteronomy, but he is convinced that in the long run autonomy cannot sustain itself. With prophetic insight he warns against the wasting of spiritual substance in modern autonomy. The concept of theonomy is healthy-minded, life-affirming, even humanistic. Perhaps there is some conflict within Tillich's thought between these two approaches to the problems of human life, but it would seem that the idea of an autonomy-affirming theonomy is the central theme. Incidentally, in connection with the cultural types, the dialectical approach would seem to be justified. In other words, an autonomous reaction is legitimate against heteronomy. However, autonomy too is finally unstable and seeks a lost theonomy.

With regard to the nature of the Christian life, Bonhoeffer's criticism raises other issues. It is clear that in Tillich's approach Christianity is a religion of salvation. At least on a superficial reading the system seems to emphasize what is done to man and to de-emphasize the demands of the Christian life. Since American Christianity has had a strong moral emphasis (to the point of moralism), this feature of the system is striking, if not disturbing, to the average American Christian. It gives the impression of being highly religious or theological but not very strongly ethical. Bonhoeffer's approach to Christianity, however, seems to identify a moral quality of the Christian life as the central concern of the gospel. The Christian must disregard his own salvation and enter into the life of the world with self-forgetting concern.

This apparent contrast brings to the fore one of the most basic theological issues which has been raised in connection with Tillich's theology. The problem may be posed initially as the question of Tillich's approach to concern with self. This area can be introduced by a further elaboration of Tillich's phrase "ultimate concern." In Tillich's usage all religion is based upon an ultimate concern. Man is naturally concerned, says Tillich, about "that which determines our being or not-being." He elaborates this point as follows:

Nothing can be of ultimate concern for us which does not have the power of threatening and saving our being. . . . Man is ultimately concerned about his being and meaning. . . . Man is infinitely concerned about the infinity to which he belongs, from which he is separated, and for which he is longing. Man is totally concerned about the totality which is his true being. . . .[19]

This understanding of man's ultimate concern leads to Tillich's understanding of estrangement. Man is estranged from that to which he belongs. Tillich states: "Man discovers *himself* when he discovers God; he discovers something that is identical with himself although it transcends him infinitely, something from which he is estranged, but from which he never has been and never can be separated."[20] Man is ultimately concerned about that from which he is estranged: the ground of his own being and meaning. We have explained how this is conceptualized in terms of potentialities within the divine life.

Salvation, then, for Tillich is "reunion": reconciliation with that from which man is estranged but with which he ought to be united. Ultimately for Tillich all estrangement is a form of

---

[19]Tillich, *Systematic Theology*, I, p. 14. Used by permission.

[20]Tillich, *Theology of Culture*, p. 10. Used by permission.

self-estrangement or self-contradiction, and all salvation is a form of self-reconciliation. Similarly, the basic meaning of love is understood to be reunion (though a form of reunion which preserves individuality). Love is a form of discovering the self in the other and discovering the oneness of self and other in God.

Tillich acknowledges that love in the New Testament sense *(agape)* has a distinctive meaning. It is universal in its scope, whereas other loves are partial and selective. Also, it "accepts the other in spite of resistance," and it "seeks the personal fulfillment of the other."[21] Yet this concern for the well-being of the other or the enemy is rooted in the recognition of "the ultimate unity of being with being within the divine ground."[22] *Agape* desires the total fulfillment of being, of which man is a part. This is seen still more clearly in Tillich's discussion of the divine *agape.* Ultimately, God's love for the world is a form of self-love. "The divine self-love includes all creatures; and proper human self-love includes everything with which man is existentially united."[23] All love, including *agape,* is the desire for reunion with the whole of which one is a part.

How does all this agree with the New Testament concept of sacrificial love? In an analysis of Tillich's ethics, Professor Paul Ramsey has argued that Tillich's understanding of love is not in agreement with the biblical concept. After suggesting that Tillich's view is derived from the monistic and idealistic philosophy of Hegel, Ramsey writes: "The model for this understanding of the inner trinitarian life of God was first drawn from human love as reunion. This is to describe love—even the love we thrust into the very heart of God—according to the basic anatomy of idolatry."[24] In other words, Ramsey maintains that Tillich views human self-love, which as a part of the fallen world is basically idolatrous, as the model for all love, even the divine love.

In Ramsey's own view the order must be reversed: Christian love must be modeled after the revelation of God's love. In

---

[21]Tillich, *Systematic Theology,* I, p. 280.
[22]*Ibid.,* p. 281.
[23]*Ibid.,* p. 282; cf. Tillich, *Systematic Theology,* III, p. 138.
[24]Ramsey, *op. cit.,* pp. 184-185. © 1962. Prentice-Hall, Inc. Used by permission.

the divine love revealed through Christ there is no self-seeking *eros*. Human love must be transformed in imitation of God. Ramsey thinks that Tillich actually follows this procedure in certain discussions of *agape* and sees human love transformed under the impact of the divine love.[25] But Ramsey is convinced that Tillich's effort to assimilate all types of love into the single conception of love as reunion is a serious theological mistake.

Ramsey has raised what is perhaps the most important theological issue in connection with Tillich's systematic construction. Tillich has sought by his approach to reconcile the humanistic and the Christian motifs. As Walter Leibrecht has suggested, Tillich's effort is to reconcile self-giving and self-realization. Leibrecht concludes that for Tillich self-realization becomes the final criterion. For Tillich, he says, all types of love are "expressions of the power of love as forms of man's self-realization. It is self-realization which is, for Tillich, the criterion in evaluating the utterances of human love."[26] Leibrecht concludes that Tillich has allowed *eros* to gain the ascendancy over *agape,* but he also writes: "The tensions between Tillich's concepts are evident; here also lies his greatness."[27] This tension is an indication of Tillich's central mission: to reconcile the Greek and the Judeo-Christian understandings of man.

Thus, according to these three critics—Dietrich Bonhoeffer, Paul Ramsey, Walter Leibrecht—Tillich's approach to love is too strongly controlled by the idea of the drive toward self-fulfillment. In this writer's judgment Christian ethics requires a delicate balance of concepts at this point. Tillich's formulation corrects those types of Christian ethics which seem to advocate a pathological self-denial and which therefore tend to favor a masochistic type of personality. But it is probable that in this process Tillich has lost some essential features in Christian self-giving. The objections cited above serve as a further corrective in the continuing debate.

---

[25]Cf. *ibid.*, pp. 193-194.

[26]Walter Leibrecht, "The Life and Mind of Paul Tillich," in *Religion and Culture: Essays in Honor of Paul Tillich,* edited by Walter Leibrecht (New York: Harper and Brothers, 1959), p. 26.

[27]*Ibid.*, p. 27.

It is interesting to note that both Tillich and Bonhoeffer seek to avoid the authoritarian or heteronomous God, but in different ways. Bonhoeffer suggests that the modern world has forced Christians to recognize what they should have known all along—that "God is weak and powerless in the world, and that is exactly the way, the only way, in which he can be with us and help us."[28] The only conquering comes through weakness, through suffering in behalf of others. The Christian conquers by sharing in this suffering. Tillich, on the other hand, preserves the "power and glory" of God even in relation to the world. God's saving power is effective in the world. This power is not used to destroy but to fulfill the world's inherent potentialities. Man draws upon the power of God even in the freedom to rebel against God. But the divine presence and power of God are most clearly *revealed* when human power and self-assertion are negated. Man's greatest self-deception is his failure to recognize that all his power is rooted in the divine power. One could hope that the Christian would not have to choose one of these formulations over the other in an absolute fashion. Perhaps through further reflection their common ground can be recognized.

---

[28]Bonhoeffer, *op. cit.*, pp. 219-220.

CHAPTER XI

Conclusions

THE PRECEDING CHAPTERS make it clear that the author, like Professor John Macquarrie, sees in Tillich's theology "the growing-point of contemporary religious thought." This does not mean that American religious thought should become Tillichian or that his method and vocabulary should be imitated. It means that he has broken new ground and pointed new directions. In so doing he has provided a great intellectual stimulus to theology: the stimulus to come to grips with the modern world, to bring theology into open encounter with the intellectual currents of the time. If American Christianity is to survive and flourish, it must in this generation become reflective and self-critical; it must cultivate theology, but a relevant, vital theology. Tillich has shown one way in which this can be done. His thought should be a point of departure as he himself urges, not a final resting place.

It may be conceded that Tillich, in fact, engages in dialogue primarily with nineteenth-century philosophy and its twentieth-century extensions. This does not substantially detract from the essential modernity of his concerns. Religious thought has not yet fully come to terms with nineteenth-century philosophy. The neoorthodox theology in its effort to return to the insights of the Protestant Reformation has left unanswered the very questions with which Tillich seeks to deal. American Christianity, even more than its European counterpart, must come to terms with Feuerbach, Marx, Darwin, Nietzsche, and Freud as well as with such twentieth-century figures as Ludwig Wittgenstein and A. J. Ayer. The fact that Tillich is more relevant to the former group than to the latter should not be disturbing.

We have noted certain barriers to an appreciation of Tillich. Primary among these is his ontological terminology. This writer is inclined to agree with Tillich that philosophy cannot be avoided in a serious theology. It may be, however, that Tillich's insights can be cast into a philosophy employing a more familiar idiom. No such translation can reduce work like Tillich's to an elementary level, but it may serve to make honest effort more rewarding.

A more basic question has to do with the enterprise of ontology itself. We have noted that Tillich does not take twentieth-century philosophical skepticism about metaphysics seriously enough. The point may be expressed differently. To what extent is Tillich's ontology a form of theology in disguise? To raise this question concerning Tillich is, of course, to raise it concerning the entire Western ontological tradition. Is philosophy's quest for the Absolute really more a reflection upon the religious insights available in the culture than a strictly philosophical inquiry? Is ontology in a Christian context, after all, a form of Christian philosophy (a phrase which Tillich shuns)? Professor Emil Brunner has suggested that the question of a Christian philosophy must be reconsidered, and he argues that such work as that of Tillich is properly designated as such.[1] We agree that a reconsideration of this matter is desirable.

This discussion simply calls attention to the fact that philosophy itself is in a state of flux, and therefore its relation to religion and theology cannot be finally fixed. Tillich has succeeded in relating theology to a particular type of ontology, but it is not at all certain that this type will predominate in philosophy in the years ahead. We live in an age of change in all areas; it is no longer safe to speak confidently of the assured results of metaphysical inquiry.

With regard to Christian doctrine, this writer is in full sympathy with Tillich's effort to reformulate the tradition in fresh

---

[1] Cf. Emil Brunner, *Truth as Encounter* (Philadelphia: Westminster Press, 1964), pp. 50-61.

and hopefully more meaningful terms. This is not a time for concern with orthodoxy or unorthodoxy; we must look for those elements in the tradition which remain meaningful in the face of the "acids of modernity." Some features of the Christian heritage no doubt are lost as far as we are concerned, but other features can be sources of great strength when they are expressed in a meaningful contemporary idiom. Whether Tillich has found such an idiom remains in part to be seen, but his effort to do so cannot fail to be significant.

This is not to say that anyone could ever appropriately believe in the system. One can only say that he has been provoked by the system to think more deeply about that to which he gives his personal commitment. The one who studies theology may find that he can believe less than before, but he is more confident about what he does believe. William Hamilton has written: "We need to reduce the area of what is believed and to lay claim upon it."[2] One can be in sympathy with the intent of this remark and still defend Tillich's system-building enterprise. Tillich is thinking through the implications of certain beliefs. We can think with him and have our beliefs challenged, enriched, and deepened.

[2]William Hamilton, *The New Essence of Christianity* (New York: Association Press, 1961), p. 30.

Tillich and the "New Theology"

MANY PEOPLE ASSUME that the Christian theologian inhabits a world circumscribed by dusty manuscripts which in time-honored fashion he translates, edits, and interprets according to strictly traditional canons. That something new could emerge from such studies would be thought a contradiction in terms. Those holding such views were unprepared for the recent news that certain young theologians were thinking new thoughts and coming up with startling conclusions. When the press reported that these men were using the phrase "the death of God" in their descriptions of contemporary experience, a furor was created that has not yet died down. Atheists and agnostics can be tolerated, of course, if they keep their peace; indeed, there may be more than a few in the pews on Sunday morning. But might not Christian theologians (who, after all, are training ministerial candidates) be reasonably expected to hold the received opinions?

In spite of the initial shock caused by these radical reappraisals of the concept of divinity, the overall effect has been salutary. A breath of fresh air has been allowed to enter where the atmosphere had grown stale. Theological attention has been turned back from peripheral to this central concern. This does not mean that the "God is dead" movement as now understood will win the day. (This writer suspects that it will not.) It means that the concept of God as traditionally conceived is no longer intellectually adequate for contemporary man. To those who say that it is impious to question God it must be replied that it is a greater impiety not to question our concepts of God in a time when they have grown irrelevant and perhaps even meaningless.

The dramatic phraseology of the "God is dead" theologians has tended to overshadow other types of reappraisal which have recently gained a hearing in theological circles. These developments are closely enough related to the attention-getting debates concerning God to be classified with them as a "new theology." In the face of these new developments it seemed worthwhile to add to this study of Tillich a substantial postscript relating Tillich's thought to the main themes of this theology. As we have seen, some critics maintain that Tillich's work is already dated— that it is oriented toward nineteenth-century questions rather than to the present. By showing the relevance of Tillich to the issues raised by the new theology, this criticism can be laid to rest.

It is possible to discern three problem areas considered in these current discussions, the first two at least partially subsidiary to the third. The central issue is the absence of God in contemporary experience. The two subsidiary questions are (1) the problem facing Christianity in the increasing secularity of modern life; and (2) the problem facing Christianity in the increasing sense of human autonomy and self-sufficiency. We shall comment upon these latter points and Tillich's contribution to them before turning to the central theme. It will serve our purposes to refer specifically to two recent books which between them reflect all of these themes: Harvey Cox, *The Secular City,* and Paul Van Buren, *The Secular Meaning of the Gospel.*

A secular man may be defined as a man for whom in a literal sense "nothing is sacred." Similarly, a secular culture is one which has little place for the sacred or the holy. A secular outlook is a point of view which sees no need for recourse to otherworldly or transcendent realities to explain or to find meaning in this world. It remains content with the finite, the observable, the commonplace; it seeks no depth, no ultimate, no infinite. The secular man is unreligious in his heart of hearts although he may observe religious customs in a vestigial way.

It would seem apparent that secularity in this sense is more common today than ever before. Over the long sweep of history men have tended to be religious, though in a variety of forms. But in modern culture the religious world view seems no more

136

than optional, and many men find it possible to say "include me out." One would suppose that all contemporary men are touched in some way by this outlook; it is a part of the prevailing climate of opinion which is inescapable. The question arises, what attitude should Christianity adopt toward this aspect of modern culture? Is secularization unambiguously evil, something that should be resisted and overcome by the church insofar as possible?

Although unsophisticated Christians might expect an unequivocal yes to this query, it is a notable fact that some of these young theologians are giving an unequivocal no, whereas certain major theologians of the older generation (among them Tillich) give a somewhat equivocal yes and no. Let us elaborate.

Those who adopt an uncompromisingly affirmative attitude toward secularization take as their point of departure the observations of Dietrich Bonhoeffer concerning "the world come of age." Developing Bonhoeffer's point that the quest for individual salvation is not the proper concern of the true Christian, the secular theology seeks in various ways to describe a "Christianity without religion." The view is presented in these writings that distinctively religious activities are relevant only when they are approached as preparation (or "rehearsal") for service in the world. Such activities (corporate worship, prayer, devotional exercises) are not self-authenticating; they must eventuate in worldly deeds of grace in order to possess any legitimacy. It is even urged that one of the meanings of Christ's life is that in him the end of religion has appeared. Thus, secularization is viewed as one aspect of man's maturity, a freedom from dependency which all men, including Christians, should welcome. This point of view is reflected in Cox's assertion that secularization "finds its roots in the biblical faith itself."[1]

Tillich's approach to the problem of the secular and the sacred (or of culture and religion), on the other hand, builds upon a distinction between religion as a specific type of activity in a given culture and religion as an irremovable function of the human spirit. In the latter sense religion is defined by Tillich

---

[1]Cox, *The Secular City*, p. 21.

as "the self-transcendence of the spirit toward what is ultimate and unconditioned in being and meaning."[2] (This is a more useful definition than the condensed phrase "ultimate concern.") We have already examined the concept of self-transcendence, and we have seen that in Tillich's view all aspects of human culture—all products of human creativity—have the characteristic of "pointing beyond themselves" to an ultimate meaning.[3] This means that "in essence" all human culture has a religious quality in Tillich's sense of the word. By the same token, there should be no need ideally for separate religious institutions and activities. The very existence of formalized religion is a mark of man's fallenness, as we have already seen.[4] Tillich then would be in sympathy with the protest of the secular theologians against the separation of the church from the world, without, however, agreeing that in the world as we know it religion as such can be removed.

Tillich's position (in the view of this writer) is more satisfactory than that associated with the unequivocal rejection of religion. Tillich accepts the secular protest against much that is false, trivial, or irrelevant in the institutional churches. Yet the realities of man's existence require religion if self-transcendence (Spiritual Presence) and community of love (Spiritual Community) are to be actualized and preserved. Formal religion is inescapable, although it must be radically criticized. In Tillich's words, "religion as the self-transcendence of life needs the religions and needs to deny them."[5] Here is a point where Tillich's "dialectical" approach stands him in good stead. Is it not true that nurture in a particular religion may eventuate in the capacity to transcend that tradition "in the direction of the truly ultimate"? Is it not further true that effective criticism of religion frequently arises among those who have grasped the ultimate in the concepts and categories of the tradition being criticized? There is no more adequate standpoint for the reformation of a religious tradition than the best insights of the tra-

---

[2]Tillich, *Morality and Beyond* (New York: Harper and Row, 1963), p. 18.
[3]Tillich, *Systematic Theology*, III, p. 99.
[4]Cf. Chapter VIII in this book.
[5]Tillich, *Systematic Theology*, III, p. 98.

dition itself. Tillich's yes and no to religion in the end is a more adequate approach than either the unequivocal yes or the un- equivocal no. To be both in his concrete tradition and beyond it is the Christian's task in our time.

The second problem area dealt with by the new theology is the increasing sense of self-sufficiency and autonomy on the part of modern man. As Dietrich Bonhoeffer points out, some theolo- gies seek to convince secure, happy individuals that they are "really unhappy and desperate" and in need of salvation. The theologians of secularity, however, argue that Christianity should rejoice in the expansion of man's self-dependence, even if this means that he no longer depends upon the church or religion for assurance. The role of the church then becomes that of pro- tecting man's newfound autonomy against new forms of depen- dency. As Cox puts it, citing the authority of Freud: "Religion is, in a sense, the neurosis of cultures; secularization corresponds to maturation."[6] The implication of Jesus' exorcising of the demons is that by eliminating infantile dependencies man is "freed to face his world matter-of-factly."[7]

The thesis that the real function of the Christian gospel is in helping to achieve human freedom is also elaborated in Van Buren's *The Secular Meaning of the Gospel*. He argues that the dominant characteristic of the life of Jesus is freedom—freedom from the past, from dependence upon authorities, from personal anxieties, freedom for service to his neighbor.[8] Moreover, the Christian professes that this freedom has proved to be "conta- gious"; the Christian gospel "is the good news of a free man who has set other men free, first proclaimed by those to whom this had happened."[9] This is for Van Buren the secular mean- ing of the gospel. It is a meaning verifiable in purely secular categories without reference to a transcendent source of power

---

[6]Cox, *op. cit.*, p. 153.

[7]*Ibid.*, p. 154.

[8]Van Buren, *The Secular Meaning of the Gospel* (New York: The Macmillan Company, 1963), pp. 123ff.

[9]*Ibid.*, p. 138.

beyond or above the finite world. The argument, then, that traditional religious attitudes of dependency are immature is a major characteristic of the new theology.

In our introduction to Tillich's system (Chapter III) we discovered the centrality of the concepts of freedom and autonomy in his thought. We noted that for Tillich the term "freedom" signifies a certain separateness or "standing alone." The drive toward individualization is an aim inherent in all being, and this drive is consummated in human individuality. In our discussion of Tillich's social philosophy (Chapter VII) we noted Tillich's favorable account of the autonomous culture. In his view man's drive to be on his own, to realize his own potentialities, to set his own standards, cannot be denied or repressed.

At the same time Tillich sees a tragic quality in human autonomy and freedom. Individuality in its own strength cannot withstand the pitfalls of aimlessness, powerlessness, alienation. Similarly, the autonomous culture tends to become sterile and spiritually empty.

The solution to the problem of alienation cannot be one which contradicts autonomy and freedom. Rather, these qualities must be fostered, supported, and preserved. This is a central aim behind Tillich's concept of "theonomy." As we have seen, Tillich distinguishes between an archaic theonomy which is prior to the achievement of individuality and a mature theonomy which lies "beyond" the autonomous development without negating it. In the latter case the theonomous individual or culture is reunited with "the power of self-transcendence," with the power which makes freedom and cultural creativity possible. A mature theonomy is an autonomy which is in unity with the creative power of the "depths" of reality.

At still another point Tillich stresses the importance of man's freedom. It has not been widely recognized that Tillich presents a reformulation of the traditional doctrine of creation. In his approach man's freedom is the decisive factor in shaping the world in which man finds himself. As we explained earlier, it is an act of man's freedom which carries the human life-world "outside" of the divine life. Actualized finitude and the whole realm of human culture "stand upon" human freedom. It is freedom which makes a thoroughgoing pantheism impossible. Thus, for Tillich man's freedom is creative; existence takes meaningful form as the result of man's creative activity. Man creates the world of meaning in which he lives.

At the same time, Tillich is not led through this emphasis on man's freedom to a chaotic relativism of meaning. Man through his free creativity seeks to fulfill "the meaning of being." Man's creativity and freedom are rooted in God's creativity and freedom; through man's freedom God's creation is completed and fulfilled. Man must therefore choose to act in accord with the inherent structures of his own being and of other beings; his freedom is not boundlessly indeterminate. Once again Tillich's approach is dialectical; he seeks to preserve creative freedom in tension with what he calls "destiny," which is rooted in the structure of being.

The theme of man functioning as the creator of meanings is introduced in Cox's *The Secular City*. Cox overlooks the fact that Tillich has developed this concept in a very subtle analysis spanning several decades, and he suggests that Tillich's analysis of meaninglessness as a threat to modern man misses the mark.[10] Man makes his own meanings, according to Cox; secular man has learned not to seek "the" meaning of existence. This analysis, however, fails to avoid the pitfall of sheer relativism. From this standpoint how is one meaning to be evaluated as in any sense superior to another?

It would seem that Tillich has struggled with the problem of transcending relativism as Cox has not. Certainly many would agree with the thelogians of secularity that the attitude of apathetic submission to the will of God is immature and inappropriate for our time. But it is not therefore necessary to accept the view that man creates meaning "out of nothing," that there are no norms or guidelines for human creativity. Tillich's effort to combine freedom and destiny (as well as dynamics and form) is a significant contribution in this area and should not be ignored.

---

[10]Cox, *op. cit.*, p. 80.

Those who see in Tillich only his emphasis upon the weakness and despair of man have focused on his analysis of "existence" to the exclusion of his analysis of "life." In Tillich's vocabulary existence is inseparable from estrangement; therefore estrangement and the consequent anxieties are inevitable. But concrete life is an ambiguous mixture of essence, existence, and fulfillment. In his analysis of life Tillich sees and emphasizes the greatness of man's creative freedom. In so doing he is a humanist in the classical Western tradition. Yet man's greatness is tragic; it is man's very greatness—his freedom—which leads to tragic disruption. Tillich does not demean man in order to prove his need for salvation. He seeks to show that man's life is tragic in its very greatness.

We now turn to the final and central issue, the absence of God in contemporary experience. It is not possible, at least in the current state of affairs, to speak of a "death of God" theological movement. Those writers who have been grouped together under this heading do not, in fact, take the same position on the crucial issues. [11] Nevertheless, it is possible and necessary to speak of a diminution of the sense of God's reality as one mark of contemporary experience. The great Jewish theologian Martin Buber described this phenomenon as the "eclipse of God."[12] All of the writers identified with the new theology are reacting to this situation in modern Western culture. What unity their work possesses derives from this common apprehension.

The prescriptions offered by these writers as cures for man's spiritual malaise are diverse and cannot be summarized here. Suffice it to say that they do not speak with one accord. On the central issue of the role of metaphysics, for example, the suggestions range from the proposal of a neo-Hegelian thought frame-

---

[11] The writers frequently grouped in this way, along with one of their major publications, are: T. J. J. Altizer, *Oriental Mysticism and Biblical Eschatology;* Gabriel Vahanian, *The Death of God;* William Hamilton, *The New Essence of Christianity;* and Paul Van Buren, *The Secular Meaning of the Gospel.*

[12] Martin Buber, *Eclipse of God* (New York: Harper and Brothers, 1952), p. 23. "Eclipse of God" carries connotations different from those contained in "death of God."

work (Altizer) to the elimination of all metaphysics whatever (Van Buren). Although a common concern for a new Christology is at least worthy of note in several of these studies, one must conclude that no one constructive direction for theological development has yet emerged.[13] The literature cited here is provocative, and it perhaps heralds some significant shift of emphasis in Christian theology. But there are as yet no clear signs indicating where this shift will lead us in the end.

In the context of these debates it is useful to take another look at Tillich's approach to the reality of God. There is some evidence that his position is being rejected without adequate understanding. Many are still tempted to conclude, like J. Heywood Thomas, that Tillich's God is "the Absolute of the metaphysicians."[14] Insofar as Tillich's view of God is rendered as "being-itself," understood as the Greek metaphysical absolute, an inadequate picture of Tillich's thought has been presented. Approached only in this way, the influence of Plato and Hegel on Tillich is seen, but the influence of Nietzsche is not seen. However, it can be established that Nietzsche's influence on Tillich was no less decisive than that of Plato and Hegel.

Our starting point for presenting Tillich's position can be this statement made by Tillich in 1952: "The decisive event which underlies the search for meaning and the despair of it in the 20th century is the loss of God in the 19th century."[15] Tillich, of course, refers to the intellectual situation in nineteenth-century Europe. He reminds us that the "death" of God was pronounced not only by Nietzsche but also by Ludwig Feuerbach and Karl Marx. In France the philosophy of Auguste Comte might have been mentioned in the same connection. In England one thinks of agnostics like Thomas Huxley who saw in the theory of evolution the death of the theistic view of the universe. In Tillich's judgment the most creative currents of philosophy in the Western world since the mid-nineteenth century have been responses of one sort or another to the

---

[13]Cf. F. Thomas Trotter, "Variations on the 'Death of God' Theme in Recent Theology," *The Journal of Bible and Religion*, XXXIII, No. 1 (January, 1965), pp. 42-48.

[14]Thomas, *op. cit.*, p. 57.

[15]Tillich, *The Courage to Be*, p. 142.

experience of God's absence. (This is especially true of the whole movement of existentialism.) Generally speaking, Christian theology did not recognize that this atheistic philosophy was a reflection of a growing situation in the whole culture, not simply the mad ravings of a few demented individuals. Tillich's whole theology can be interpreted as an effort to meet this challenge—an effort to formulate a doctrine of God which would recognize the legitimate features of the protest against traditional theism.

We have already sketched the main lines of Tillich's concept of God. More needs to be said, however, concerning the influence of Nietzsche upon Tillich's formulations. For Tillich finds in Nietzsche the most effective expression of the philosophy of life;[16] and he finds in an analysis of courage along Nietzschean lines "an outstanding key for the ontological approach to reality."[17]

Nietzsche held that modern Western man must transcend Christianity (i.e., he must rise above it, not fall below it). The radical drive toward truthfulness engendered by Christianity itself requires that Christian conceptions be recognized as historically conditioned. The radical recognition of an unconditional moral demand requires that Christian morality be overcome. Even Nietzsche's exhortation to man to surpass himself, to create the "Overman," seems to root partially in a religious dissatisfaction with anything finite. In the place of the infinite God Nietzsche proclaims the self-surpassing man reaching toward the infinite. Thus, in the philosophy of Nietzsche Christian motives negate Christian contents. Perhaps referring in part to Christianity, he writes: "All great things perish by themselves, by an act of self-abrogation."[18]

It is clear that Tillich's concept of self-transcendence owes much to Nietzsche's description of the self-surpassing man. Fur-

---

[16]*Ibid.*, p. 27.

[17]*Ibid.*, p. 31.

[18]Friedrich Nietzsche, *Collected Works*, Vol. VII, p. 482, quoted in Karl Jaspers, *Nietzsche and Christianity*, trans. by E. B. Ashton (New York: Henry Regnery Company, A Gateway Edition, 1961), p. 83. The above account of Nietzsche is dependent upon Jaspers' interesting analysis.

thermore, Tillich is convinced that this drive in man is fundamentally religious in character. Tillich finds in Nietzsche (and in
others like him) an ultimate seriousness which, he believes, can
only stem from a sense of ultimacy. Nietzsche's impulse to push
beyond everything finite (including a finite God) is his "ultimate
concern," a concern which is implicitly, though not explicitly,
religious.

In this context Tillich raises the question of the "power"
to transcend finitude. Nietzsche uses the phrase "the will to
power" to describe man's basic drive toward self-transcendence.
Tillich comments: "Nietzsche's will to power is neither will nor
power. . . . It designates the self-affirmation of life as life, including self-preservation and growth."[19] It is this power of self-
affirmation which overcomes the negative aspects of finitude.
Tillich adds the further point that a power which overcomes
the negativities of finitude cannot be a finite power; it cannot itself be subject to the limitations which it overcomes. The power
that enables us to reach beyond finitude must be itself beyond
the limitations of finitude.

The Christian of our time, like Nietzsche, is driven by an
ultimate seriousness to doubt the concrete symbols for God of his
tradition. Tillich affirms that this very concern, this very urge
to transcend limitation in the direction of true ultimacy, is itself
rooted in the power of that reality to which the symbols in-
adequately pointed. The God who is the power of self-transcendence is for Tillich the God beyond the God of theism. In a
phrase which Paul Schilling applies to Rudolf Bultmann, God is
"the power which frees man from finitude."[20] Ultimately for
Tillich it is the reality of man's freedom which forces us to speak
of a power beyond finite nature (at least beyond nature as
known by man in the subject-object relationship).

The key to Tillich's relation to naturalism would seem to lie
in his rather ambiguous distinction between two forms of self-

[19]Tillich, *The Courage to Be*, pp. 26-27.
[20]Paul Schilling, *Contemporary Continental Theologians* (New York: Abingdon Press, 1966), p. 84.

transcendence. First, there is natural self-transcendence, which might be referred to broadly as the life-force. This force drives beyond all finite forms but nevertheless remains tragic in its inability to gain infinitude. There is, however, another possibility: "ecstatic" self-transcendence, whereby man is elevated beyond the tragic aspects of finitude. The latter is the result of grace, not nature, in Tillich's conceptualization. He has never fully clarified the relationship betwen the two possibilities; the one seems to rise, phoenix-like, from the self-abnegation of the other. The question as to whether there is an essential continuity between tragic natural self-transcendence and successful ecstatic self-transcendence seems to this writer to be a fundamental unresolved issue in Tillich's theology.[21]

This analysis of the power of successful self-transcendence is Tilich's version of the doctrine of the Holy Spirit. The Spirit of God is in our efforts to reach God, giving us in a fragmentary way what we seek. Yet the tragic quality of life remains. Men do not possess infinitude. But we can glimpse it and in moments of genuine self-transcendence share in it. We are "in God" (and united with one another) when we are "above" ourselves. Tillich attempts to teach us not to conceptualize God as a being above us toward whom we reach upward. We do indeed rise above ourselves in moments of grace or "ecstasy" (in Tillich's sense). But this is not an ascent "toward" God. Figuratively speaking it is "toward" greater freedom, openness, love *(agape)*, creative life. This is achieved, however, in the power of the Spirit. "Where the Spirit of the Lord is, there is freedom" (2 Cor. 3:17). What we think of as reaching for God is really a quest for infinitude. But this is done in the power of the Spirit.

Tillich does not claim that this ontology of self-transcendence and courage is a sufficient basis for Christian theology. Religion also needs concrete symbols drawn from historical tradition. Meaningful symbols grow and die; perhaps we find ourselves in a period of the death of symbols. But it would seem that Tillich's

---

[21]Cf. my discussion of this matter in Hammond, *op cit.*, pp. 109-111; 160-170; 177-179.

analysis of the power of self-transcendence is helpful as a tentative formulation of that to which the symbols point. This suggestion of a self-transcending naturalism in the place of classical theism deserves the consideration of those who find themselves living in a time of the "death of God." Tillich's theology was written specifically for this time.

Bibliography

PART I:

Books and articles referred to in this study

Altizer, T. J. J. *Oriental Mysticism and Biblical Eschatology.* Philadelphia: Westminster Press, 1961.

Ayer, A. J. *Language, Truth, and Logic.* New York: Dover Publications, Inc., 1946.

Bergson, Henri. *Creative Evolution.* New York: Modern Library, 1944.

Bonhoeffer, Dietrich. *Letters and Papers from Prison.* New York: The Macmillan Company, 1962.

Brauer, Jerald C. Eulogy. *Criterion,* V, No. 1 (1966), p. 21.

Brunner, Heinrich Emil. *Truth as Encounter.* Philadelphia: Westminister Press, 1964.

Buber, Martin. *The Eclipse of God.* New York: Harper and Row, A Harper Torchbook, 1957.

Cox, Harvey. *The Secular City.* New York: The Macmillan Company, 1965.

de Chardin, Pierre T. *The Phenomenon of Man.* New York: Harper and Row, A Harper Torchbook, 1961.

Edwards, Paul. "Professor Tillich's Confusions," *Mind,* LXXIV, No. 294 (April, 1965), pp. 206-214.

Hamilton, Kenneth. *The System and the Gospel.* New York: The Macmillan Company, 1963.

Hamilton, William. *The New Essence of Christianity.* New York: Association Press, 1961.

Hammond, G. B. *Man in Estrangement.* Nashville: Vanderbilt University Press, 1965.

Hordern, William. *Speaking of God.* New York: The Macmillan Company, 1964.

Jaspers, Karl. *Nietzsche and Christianity.* New York: Henry Regnery Company, A Gateway Edition, 1961.

Kegley, Charles W. and Robert W. Bretall (eds.). *The Theology of Paul Tillich.* New York: The Macmillan Company, 1952.

Leibrecht, Walter (ed.). *Religion and Culture: Essays in Honor of Paul Tillich.* New York: Harper and Brothers, 1959.

Macquarrie, John. *Twentieth Century Religious Thought.* New York: Harper and Row, 1963.

Martin, Bernard. *The Existentialist Theology of Paul Tillich.* New York: Bookman Associates, 1963.

Marty, Martin E. and Dean G. Peerman (eds.). *New Theology No. 1.* New York: The Macmillan Company, 1964.

Miller, Perry. *Jonathan Edwards.* New York: Meridian Books, 1959.

Niebuhr, Reinhold. "Paul Tillich in Memoriam," *Union Seminary Quarterly Review,* XXI, No. 1 (Nov., 1965), p. 11.

Pauck, Wilhelm. "The Sources of Paul Tillich's Richness," *Union Seminary Quarterly Review,* XXI, No. 1 (November, 1965), pp. 3-9.

Ramsey, Paul. *Nine Modern Moralists.* Englewood Cliffs, N. J.: Prentice-Hall, Inc., 1962.

Randall, John Herman, Jr. *The Role of Knowledge in Western Religion.* Boston: Starr King Press, 1958.

Robinson, John A. T. *Honest to God*. Philadelphia: Westminster Press, 1963.

Rome, Sidney and Beatrice Rome (eds.). *Philosophical Interrogations*. New York: Holt, Rinehart and Winston, 1964.

Schilling, S. Paul. *Contemporary Continental Theologians*. New York: Abingdon Press, 1966.

Schweitzer, Albert. *The Quest for the Historical Jesus*. New York: The Macmillan Company, 1948.

Tavard, George H. *Paul Tillich and the Christian Message*. New York: Charles Scribner's Sons, 1962.

—————. "Paul Tillich's System," *The Commonweal*, LXXIX (February 7, 1964), p. 566.

Thomas, J. Heywood. *Paul Tillich: An Appraisal*. Philadelphia: The Westminster Press, 1963.

Tillich, Paul. *The Courage to Be*. New Haven: Yale University Press, 1952.

—————. *The Dynamics of Faith*. New York: Harper and Brothers, A Harper Torchbook, 1958.

—————. "Estrangement and Reconciliation in Modern Thought," *Review of Religion*, IX (November, 1944), pp. 5-19.

—————. *The Eternal Now*. New York: Charles Scribner's Sons, 1963.

—————. *Morality and Beyond*. New York: Harper and Row, 1963.

—————. *The New Being*. New York: Charles Scribner's Sons, 1955.

—————. *The Protestant Era*. Translated by James Luther Adams. Chicago: The University of Chicago Press, 1948.

—————. *The Shaking of the Foundations*. New York: Charles Scribner's Sons, 1948.

——————. *Systematic Theology,* Vol. I. Chicago: The University of Chicago Press, 1951.

——————. *Systematic Theology,* Vol. II. Chicago: The University of Chicago Press, 1957.

——————. *Systematic Theology,* Vol. III. Chicago: The University of Chicago Press, 1963.

——————. *Theology of Culture.* Ed. Robert C. Kimball. New York: Oxford University Press, 1959.

Trotter, F. Thomas. "Variations on the 'Death of God' Theme in Recent Theology," *The Journal of Bible and Religion,* XXXIII, No. 1 (January, 1965), pp. 42-48.

Vahanian, Gabriel. *The Death of God.* New York: George Braziller, 1961.

Van Buren, Paul. *The Secular Meaning of the Gospel.* New York: The Macmillan Company, 1963.

——————. "Tillich as Apologist," a review of *Paul Tillich: An Appraisal* by J. Heywood Thomas, *The Christian Century,* 81, No. 6 (February 5, 1964), p. 177.

Whitehead, A. N. *Science and the Modern World.* New York: The Macmillan Company, 1925.

PART II

Annotated Bibliography

A. Selected works by Tillich

Tillich, Paul. *The Shaking of the Foundations.* New York: Charles Scribner's Sons, 1948.

——————. *The New Being.* New York: Charles Scribner's Sons, 1955.

——————. *The Eternal Now.* New York: Charles Scribner's Sons, 1963. The above are three collections of Tillich's sermons, reflecting the depth and breadth of his

Christian experience but in terms comprehensible to laymen.

Brown, D. Mackensie. *Ultimate Concern: Tillich in Dialogue.* New York: Harper and Row, 1965. Tape recording of Tillich talking with students, faculty, and clergy. A good way to be introduced to the man and his thought.

Tillich, Paul. *The Protestant Era.* Chicago: The University of Chicago Press, 1948. (Abridged edition, A Phoenix Paperback, 1957.) A collection of Tillich's essays from the earlier period, including his comments on the fate of Protestantism, the meaning of history, religion and culture, etc. Includes two introductions: one by Tillich himself and one by the translator, James Luther Adams.

——————. *Morality and Beyond.* New York: Harper and Row, 1963. A somewhat condensed but nevertheless readable introduction to Tillich's ethics. From the aspect of ethics, the best introduction to the system as a whole for the general reader. Includes two essays from *The Protestant Era.*

——————. *Theology of Culture.* Edited by Robert C. Kimball. New York: Oxford University Press, 1959. Important essays from the later period. Includes Tillich's analysis of existentialism and of psychoanalysis.

——————. *Biblical Religion and the Search for Ultimate Reality.* Chicago: The University of Chicago Press, A Phoenix Paperback, 1964. An excellent introduction to the problem of relating the Bible to Western philosophy.

——————. *The Dynamics of Faith.* New York: Harper and Brothers, 1957. Stimulating analysis of what faith is and is not. Challenging but manageable for the layman.

——————. *Christianity and the Encounter of the World Religions.* New York: Columbia University Press, 1963. One of Tillich's less substantial and therefore more readable books on an important contemporary theme. Special consideration of Buddhism.

—————. *The Courage to Be.* New Haven: Yale University Press, 1952. (Yale Paperback, 1959.) For the student of philosophy this is Tillich's most important single work. Difficult but rewarding for the reader with some philosophical (or perhaps psychological) background.

—————. *Love, Power, and Justice.* New York: Oxford University Press, A Galaxy Book, 1960. An analysis which shows how these moral qualities are rooted in fundamental metaphysical realities. Tillich's social philosophy.

—————. *The Religious Situation.* New York: Meridian Books, Inc., 1956. Of interest to students of twentieth-century European history. Somewhat less valuable for the general reader.

—————. *The Interpretation of History.* Part I, translated by N. A. Rasetzki; parts II, III, and IV translated by Elsa L. Talmey. New York: Charles Scribner's Sons, 1936. Tillich's discussion of such themes as the relation of eternity to time (the *kairos* concept) and the demonic in history.

—————. *Systematic Theology,* Vol. I. Chicago: University of Chicago Press, 1951. Indispensable for any thorough understanding of Tillich. Full elaboration of his concepts of reason and revelation, being-itself and God. Assumes some philosophical and theological background.

—————. *Systematic Theology,* Vol. II. Chicago: University of Chicago Press, 1957. Tillich's existentialist analysis of man and his approach to the doctrine of Christ. Can be read independently of Vol. I and is somewhat less demanding.

—————. *Systematic Theology,* Vol. III. Chicago: University of Chicago Press, 1963. Tillich's approach to the ambiguities of life and their resolution in the life of the spirit, the ambiguities of history and their resolution in the kingdom of God. Provocative but puzzling without prior knowledge of Tillich's thought. Contains his fullest discussion of the nature of the church.

—————. *The World Situation*. Philadelphia: Fortress Press, A Facet Book, 1965. Short pamphlet reprinting a 1945 essay. An attempt to find meaning in the trends of twentieth-century history. Critique of *laissez faire* capitalism and aspects of liberal democracy.

—————. *The Future of Religions*. New York: Harper and Row, 1966. Posthumous collection of four of Tillich's last lectures. Includes several tributes and a collection of photographs.

B. Studies of Tillich's work

Adams, James Luther. *Tillich's Philosophy of Science, Culture, and Religion*. New York: Harper and Row, 1965. Best study of Tillich's early German works. Shows his thought in formative stages. Rather difficult for the general reader. Bibliography through 1945.

Hamilton, Kenneth. *The System and the Gospel*. New York: The Macmillan Company, 1963. A sharply critical study of the System as a whole. Stimulating if not finally convincing.

Hammond, Guyton B. *Man in Estrangement: A Comparison of the Thought of Paul Tillich and Erich Fromm*. Nashville, Tenn.: Vanderbilt University Press, 1965. An analysis which sheds new light on Tillich's concepts of God, freedom, and the relation between God and the world.

Kegley, Charles W., and Robert W. Bretall (eds.). *The Theology of Paul Tillich*. New York: Macmillan, 1952. Best collection of critical articles to date, but limited to the works written before 1952. Autobiographical essay by Tillich included. Bibliography.

Leibrecht, Walter (ed.). *Religion and Culture: Essays in Honor of Paul Tillich.* New York: Harper and Brothers, 1959. Helpful introduction to Tillich's life and thought by the editor, and extensive Tillich bibliography.

McKelway, Alexander J. *The Systematic Theology of Paul Tillich.* Richmond, Virginia: John Knox Press, 1964. Helpful as a one-volume synopsis of the System.

Martin, Bernard. *The Existentialist Theology of Paul Tillich.* New York: Bookman Associates, 1963. A helpful introduction to Tillich's concepts of reason, revelation, man, estrangement, and the New Being by a Jewish scholar. Best digest of these parts of the System for the general reader. Biographical information included.

O'Meara, Thomas A., O. P., and Celestin D. Weisser, O. P. (eds.). *Paul Tillich in Catholic Thought.* Dubuque, Iowa: The Priory Press, 1964. Essays on Tillich's thought by a group of Catholic scholars which shed light on Tillich and on current trends in Catholic theology.

Tavard, George H. *Paul Tillich and the Christian Message.* New York: Charles Schribner's Sons, 1962. An analysis of Tillich's Christology by a Catholic scholar. Criticism of Tillich from the standpoint of Protestant as well as Catholic orthodoxy. Biographical information included.

Thomas, J. Heywood. *Paul Tillich: An Appraisal.* Philadelphia: The Westminster Press, 1963. A critique of Tillich from the standpoint of linguistic philosophy. Tends to be piecemeal in its approach and overlooks important Tillichian conceptions. Biographical information included.

Index

156

Index

(1)